GW00857885

Passionate Pursuit

28 KEYS TO UNLOCK YOUR DREAM

MJ Spanswick

XULON PRESS ELITE

Xulon Press Elite
2301 Lucien Way #415
Maitland, FL 32751
407.339.4217
www.xulonpress.com

© 2020 by MJ Spanswick

All rights reserved solely by the author. The author guarantees all contents are original and do not infringe upon the legal rights of any other person or work. No part of this book may be reproduced in any form without the permission of the author. The views expressed in this book are not necessarily those of the publisher.

Unless otherwise indicated, Scripture quotations taken from the New American Standard Bible (NASB). Copyright © 1960, 1962, 1963, 1968, 1971, 1972, 1973, 1975, 1977, 1995 by The Lockman Foundation. Used by permission. All rights reserved.

Printed in the United States of America.

ISBN-13: 978-1-6312-9080-0

Table of Contents

Introduction

If you have ever wondered about doing something different in your life, if you have a desire or a dream that you want to fulfill but don't know how to start or are feeling overwhelmed just thinking about it, or are even fearful of setting out on the adventure, then this is the book for you.

Passionate Pursuit will help you to gain the confidence to step out and make that start. If you have started but come across problems, then this book will help you to keep going in the right direction and not give up.

Most of us, when we're young, do not know what our divine destiny is; I certainly didn't and I pursued my dreams and adventures (and some of my husband's) just because they seemed good to do at the time. A few of those dreams changed the lives of others, but they all impacted mine. Only now as I look back, I can see how those dreams and my career in project management for over thirty years have converged to the point of writing this book. My desire for this book is that it will empower you to achieve your dream, which may then put you on destiny's path for your life.

We've all heard the Frank Sinatra song "My Way." Well, this is your chance to do it *your way*.

There are twenty-eight keys in this book; each has been divided into four sections. The first is motivational quotes and the second is a song that fits with the chapter's theme. In the third portion, I normally share an experience from my life, with narrative that applies that illustration. The fourth section is the most important: which are questions/actions to apply the key to *your* life and dream. You may be able to answer some of these questions straight away, whilst others may need time to ponder. Either way, take the time to write down the answers. Some of the appendices will be downloadable in native format at www.mjspanswick.com so that you can adapt them for your dream. Also at the website, there will be a section to let me know your dream and how the book helped you.

In fact, congratulations! Because by reading this book, you have already taken your first step on the path to accomplish your dream.

Let's keep going!

Two roads diverged in a wood, and I,
I took the one less traveled by,
And that has made all the difference.

Excerpt from "The Road Not Taken"
by Robert Frost (1874- 1963)

"I have a dream..."
–Martin Luther King

"This is the beginning of anything you want"
– Unknown

1

Tell me your dream

"You got to have a dream, If you don't have a dream, How you gonna have a dream come true?"
Happy Talk – South Pacific, Rodgers and Hammerstein

All of us dream of something; sometimes we don't remember the dreams that we have at night, but we all have dreams inside of us that we would like to achieve; whether it's to own your own home, a sports car, start your own business, write a book, be popular or of doing something heroic.

If your imagination was set free, where would it go? Aim for the stars.

Some people keep that dream with them all their lives, never even trying to fulfill it, and so they never realize that dream.

Jordan Peterson is quoted as saying, "It is your duty to follow your purpose." Is your dream part of your purpose or destiny? I believe they are often closely connected, and that even if you pursue your dream and it isn't your purpose, it may lead you to it.

My husband, Jon, and I have had the privilege of following several of our dreams, most of them whilst having busy day jobs. Some took more time than others, some took more detailed planning, and some you will hear about later on. We have built a replica of a 1937 Jaguar SS100; we have kitted out a Land Rover and driven all the way from South Africa back to the UK, covering nineteen countries and three continents. We ran a half marathon only three months after I ran my first one km. We have trekked up some of the highest mountains in Africa and some high passes in the Himalayas. When in Thailand, we set up a small business to teach and employ ex-sex workers to sew, so they didn't need to sell their bodies in order to feed their children. We are currently in the process of restoring a twelfth century chateau in the south of France, and now I can add becoming an author to my list. We have met many new friends along the way, as well as learned lots of new skills. Some of our dreams touched the lives of others, but all of our dreams changed ours.

Each of us has a purpose and a destiny in this life; you may not even know what that purpose is at the moment. But by following your dream, you may also find your purpose like I did.

One thing to note: Don't ever be afraid of running out of dreams as you will find that once you complete one, your eyes will be opened to other dreams to fulfill.

1. Do you have a desire or a dream in this life that you wish to pursue?

2. Create your bucket list of things that you'd like to achieve before it's too late.

3. What is stopping you from pursuing your dream(s)?

Then the Lord answered me and said, "Record the vision and inscribe it on tablets, that the one who reads it may run,"
Habakkuk 2:2.

"Some people dream of success, while other people get up every morning and make it happen"
– Wayne Huizenga

"Potential is worth nothing if it's not used"
– Rene Treeyanon

2

Tell me your goal

"Que será, será, Whatever will be, will be, The future's not ours to see, que será, será."
"Que Será, Será"–Doris Day

Y ou might be thinking, "Didn't we do this one yesterday, when we talked about dreams?" The answer is Yes, we talked about your dreams yesterday but we didn't talk about your goals. There is something very different psychologically between a dream and a goal, and that difference is *intentionality*.

The majority of people in this life stay in their comfort zones for all of their days, they don't try to stretch themselves. They may not even like what they are doing, but it's safe, it's normal, and nothing changes until they are jolted out of that thinking. We were the same way.

We had both been working for the same engineering company in the UK for twelve years. We had known others who had been given sabbaticals (unpaid time off) for up to a year. We wanted to travel around Australia and New Zealand, but with those locations being so far away, wanted to take three months out. With all of our holidays from one year, Christmas and all the holidays from the next year, we only needed a couple of weeks unpaid, so we didn't think it would be a problem. Unfortunately, our boss was new to the role and so asked the human resource (HR) department for guidance. HR said that we would have to resign. We were utterly astounded. We had been there for twelve years, had good reputations, and were both due to finish on our respective projects a few weeks before Christmas. Our astonishment turned to anger and we decided that if we were going to have to resign, then we would do a bigger adventure to make it worthwhile. Jon had always had a dream to travel the length of Africa and loved Land Rovers so we decided that we would take a year out, but would resign when it suited us. We spent the next three years saving up and planning the details. We both agree that it was the best year of our lives and since then, we have been quicker to follow our dreams.

We all know people who have a dream of doing something, or being someone, but when you ask them what they are doing to make that dream become a reality, the answer is basically nothing. There are many people who could make a difference in this world but don't.

I will cover some of the blockages that stop people later in this book, but here is the first.

People don't make their dream their goal.

It's as if they just expect it to happen, "Que será, será, what will be, will be…." Unfortunately for those people, the probability is that it will never happen, and their dream will just remain a dream.

But the good news is that as you are reading this book, you already have intentionality of making something happen.

I believe that we all have a destiny and good plan for our lives, but we also have to be willing to walk it out, it will not just fall onto our laps.

Every decision we make in life has a consequence and whether you realize it or not, inaction is also a decision, with the consequence of nothing happening.

The first step in making your dream your goal is to take it from the realm of the imagination and to bring it into reality and as the quote above says, "Record the vision and inscribe it on tablets" in other words write it down. Change it from being ethereal to being tangible. Once written, it can be seen and clarified as necessary. It's simple really, to achieve your goal, you need to know what it is.

Once you have written it down, tell a few trusted friends, because by doing that you are starting to commit to it. And then start to expand upon it; is it something that you will be doing on your own or in a group? Is it something that you want to make into a career or just do for fun?

In the quote for Chapter 1, Martin Luther King starts out by telling us that he has a dream but he didn't stop there. In his speech, he tells us what that dream was and he made it a goal by pursuing it and the rest is history.

There is a big difference between saying, "I could have done something" and saying "I did do something."

1. Fill out the Dream Questionnaire at the back of the book. Then once you have answered the questions, get a blank piece of paper and write out in your own words what your dream and goal is. Write as much detail as you can.

2. How will you define success for your goal?

"As a man thinketh in his heart, so is he,"
Proverbs 23:7.

"I am not like everyone else, I don't pretend to be, I don't want to be, I am me,"
-Agapo.

3

Who are you now?

"Raindrops on roses and whiskers on kittens... I simply remember my favorite things, and then I don't feel so bad."
"My Favorite Things"–*The Sound of Music*–Rogers and Hammerstein

"Let Me Be Myself"
–3 Doors Down

I was born the youngest of five children: three boys, then two girls, and if you believe my mother, we were all mistakes; however, I'd like to think that we were all miracles instead. Being the youngest, you soon get used to hearing, "Oh you are so and so's (pick one of the other four) sister" and depending on whether the four elder siblings were good or bad, you tend to get pre-judged and tarred with the same brush. However, when it was time to go to senior school (age eleven), I managed to get a grant (partial scholarship) to go to the grammar school twelve miles away. I guess that I sort of assumed that everyone knew that I was the youngest of five because they always had known till that point and several of the teachers were acquainted with the family. However, when I was in my third year there, I was talking to a good friend about my family, she suddenly turned around to me and said, "I didn't know that you had any brothers and sisters, I thought you were an only child!" I was shocked (so much that even today, that memory is really vivid) and it was only then that I realized that I was being judged on my own merits; that they either liked me or didn't like me, based solely on who I was as an individual. That was quite an eye-opener for me.

The title of this chapter may seem like a strange question, but just as you have to decide where you are going with your dream and where you are starting from, you also need to take stock of "Who am I?" Different psychologists have differing ideas as to what affects who you are, some think it's nature – i.e. your parents and grandparents had this DNA and so that is what you are, whilst others believe that it is your nurture – i.e. how you were brought up that affects who you are. There are published books that will tell you how you will act depending on whether you were a single/ oldest child or whether you were the youngest of many. Leaders statistically are more likely to be single/oldest and comedians the youngest. However, just because there is a trend, doesn't mean that you can't be the exception to the rule. I was the youngest of five siblings, so in theory, I should be the comedienne vying for the attention of the others by cracking jokes, etc., but my memories of us all around the dinner table was the middle sibling, Damian, being the one that cracked the jokes and made us all laugh.

Personally, I believe it to be a mix, but not only of nature and nurture but also of *whom you determine yourself to be*.

All of the above things put together in a package called *you* means that there is no one else like you in this world. You are unique and special.

This is being borne out by the research of neuro-scientists such as Dr. Caroline Leaf who came up with the notion of neuro plasticity – i.e. we can change the neuro connections in our brains. For example, if you think positive thoughts, then you can change your mood to be happy. This is something that Rogers and Hammerstein had discovered prior to writing "My Favorite Things" for the *Sound of Music* (and that God noted in the bible thousands of years earlier). The point is that we have to *want* to change. Even with the simple example of being happy, you need to take every negative thought captive and change it to a positive thought. "Finally brethren, whatever is true, whatever is honorable, whatever is right, whatever is pure, whatever is lovely, whatever is of good repute, if there is any excellence, and anything worthy of praise, dwell on these things" Philippians 4:8.

We have all been born with natural gifts and talents (yes, even those of you reading this now thinking – I haven't got any/ I don't know what they are). Sometimes we know what these are i.e. we know that we are good at mathematics or languages, but sometimes we have gifts that are within our blind spots and it helps to get a good friend to tell us what qualities they see in us. You may be a good encourager, or someone who can teach others, or be able to condense down complex situations to something more understandable.

Don't pigeon-hole yourself with how others have labeled you, whether this was by your family or teachers or friends. Also, don't be limited by your current job title, even if it's a good title. It may not be what you were called to be.

Another way would be to go online to a website like www.16personalities.com and do a free online questionnaire which will then tell you your personality traits, strengths and weaknesses.

Of course, that isn't the end of it. Once you have a better understanding of what has and hasn't shaped your life into who you are now, and what gifts and talents you have, the next step is to look back at what you want to do. My guess is that if you have a passion for something, then it is most likely linked to your destiny (unless of course your passion is to sit on a couch eating lots of chocolate; then you may need to stretch yourself a bit!).

1. Make a list of your gifts and talents.

2. List what you think your weaknesses are.

3. Ask a good friend to tell you what they think your strengths are.

4. Once listed, consider how you can you use your strengths to help you achieve your dream.

"Imagine who you could be and aim single mind-edly at that"
— Jordan Peterson

"The only person you are destined to become is the person you decide to be."
— Ralph Waldo Emerson.

"We can't become what we want by remaining who we are."
— Rich Dad Quotes

4

Who do you need to be?

"Who I'm meant to be"
–Anthem Lights

We talked earlier about who you are at the moment, so the next step is, how does that fit with what you want to do and where you want to go? In other words, who do you need to be to achieve your goal? Now don't start to believe the lie that I am what I am and there's no changing me, there is always an ability to change, *if* you so desire. Think of it as investing in your future.

In 2002, I was sent to Pattaya, Thailand by the engineering firm that Jon and I worked for in the UK to add some Project Management expertise to the daughter company there. We were promised that they would transfer Jon across as soon as there was a suitable position. Unfortunately, this took nine months, but in that time, I became good friends with some women, two

17

of which, Nella and Eve, ran a ministry that helped sex-workers start a new life by giving them inner healing and new practical life skills so that they could earn a living another way. Sometime after Jon arrived, Nella told me that they had been given four industrial sewing machines and wondered if I knew any small business that would like to partner with them to teach the girls to sew. What she didn't know was that we had been wondering about making a bedcover out of Thai silk as we hadn't been able to find one, and were therefore wondering if this was a business opportunity. However, having always worked for a large firm, we had absolutely no experience of setting up or running our own company, especially in a foreign country where we didn't speak the language. We decided to give it a go (with the engineering company's permission as we still intended on working full time for them as well). It was a steep learning curve – the first thing we did was employ a trained seamstress to teach the girls to sew and who would supervise their work. Then we frantically set about learning all about branding, packaging, design, websites, internet selling and the rest including sourcing all the materials. We read lots of books and asked anyone we knew who had relevant experience for advice and help. I tell people now that I may not have the letters behind my name, but it was better than any MBA I could have done in college.

So, if who you are now doesn't fit with whom you need to be (note 'need' not necessarily 'want') in order for you to be successful at what you want to do, then what are the gaps? For example: if you want to be a fashion designer, you are going to need some skills, such as being able to draw – so that you can see what it is you are going to create, you need to understand fabrics and the different ways they react being cut with or against the bias, and how they will fall. You need to be able to make patterns, so that people can take these and manufacture against them, and you need to be able to sew, in order to create your original master-piece. Now some of these you will be able to outsource, but which ones are you going to do?

So, if you haven't got the skills you need, how are you going to get them? The first one would be going back to school. Now some of you may say, 'Yes, but I already have a full-time job, which I need to continue with. Well, could you look at evening classes at a local college or open university or even enroll for courses on-line which allow you to study in your own time. Likewise, read books written by people who have done it before, if you can't afford to buy them, then try bor-rowing them from your local library.

When it comes to training, try and work out *how* you learn. Personally, I am a visual learner; when I used to have exams at school, I would remember how it looked on the page and what doodle it was next to. Now when I recall a meeting, I see how the room was set up, and who was sitting where when they said something.

If you are an audio learner, then as you are remembering something you will probably hear it in your mind. One way to help you revise would be to speak it out loud or record it and listen to it over and over again. If this is you, then see what podcasts are available on-line that can help. The other aspect of this is how are you best taught? Are you best on your own i.e. you get the books and tools and teach yourself, in which case, why not explore what how-to videos there are on-line? We recently visited Jon's sister whose partner has just bought a small holding and a few animals. Whilst there, he was expertly inoculating the sheep. I asked him where he had been trained, to which his response was that he'd learnt everything by watching YouTube videos (I was very impressed)!

Or are you best in the classroom when you have a teacher explaining it, or with a group of peers who do self-help? (Check out Facebook groups and other web forums where you can exchange questions and ideas.) Are you a self-motivator or do you need to be pushed? If you are the latter, then find someone to whom you can be accountable; if you can afford a coach or mentor, then brilliant, if not, then just find a friend who's going to ask you how you are getting on with your project. This helps keep you on track, especially if you have made a plan which you can then share with them so they know how far you should have gotten. As I write this book, I'm also trying to improve my French, ready to live at the chateau. So I asked a French teacher at one of the local schools to tutor me. Having that one hour a week keeps me in check as I know that I have to do my homework and it keeps me accountable. I know that if I didn't have it, then I would let my French slip, as there is always something else that needs doing.

1. What extra skills do you need to be successful in your dream?

2. Which method of learning suits you best?

3. What is the best method for you to attain these skills?

4. If you have more than one skill to learn, which skill will you need first?

Person 1: Can you tell me how to get to the station?
Person 2: Yes, but I wouldn't start from here.

5

Where are you now?

"Let's start at the very beginning, a very good place to start"
"Do-Re-Mi"–*The Sound of Music*–Rodgers and
Hammerstein

U nfortunately, we don't have the luxury of being able to decide to start from somewhere else. You are unique and have your own sovereign beginnings. Each of us has a destiny and a purpose, it has been written in the stars. You have been given gifts and talents that only you have so you won't be able to do it exactly as 'so and so' did, each journey is unique. We are now living in a time like no other, the possibilities are endless.

Depending on what your dream is, the physical location where you are may or may not matter. For instance, if you want to make a round the world trip, it doesn't matter where you start from, but if you want to help the poor in Africa in a practical way, then it's better to have "boots on the ground". Sometimes you may not even come across your dream until you are in a certain location and see the need. Just like us, we didn't go to Pattaya, Thailand with an idea of helping sex-workers escape from that life, we were sent as engineers to design oil refineries and petrochemical plants. However once there, we saw the need to give these women new skills, as well as a possible business opportunity.

Trying to do things long distance may not be impossible, but it can make it a lot more difficult and take longer to implement. We know this first hand as we are living in Kuwait trying to renovate a chateau in France. Time is limited to working on it during holidays or by getting tradesmen in to do the work; although we have found that they are more likely to turn up if they know that you are going to be there, or coming very soon after. However, as I said, *more difficult* is not *impossible*, but the lack of time to do it needs to be taken into account in both your schedule and your expectations. With us, we know that it won't get finished properly until we are there full time.

Now you are not going to find the North Pole if you haven't got a passport and don't want to leave your home town. However, if you want to set up a business, then your home town may be the best place to do it as you will have the contacts to help you and will know the local customs and laws (something we had to learn in Thailand).

The other question is: Where are you psychologi-cally? I realize that at certain times of our lives, we are unable to cope with one more thing to worry about. If that's you, that's fine, give yourself time to get through that phase. But don't leave it too late to start, your *bucket list* is best done throughout your life rather than waiting for the doctor's notification of a deadly disease.

If you feel ready for a challenge but still have a few fears, then don't worry as we cover how to overcome fear in Chapter 11.

1. Where are you physically?

2. Is this where you need to be? If not, what action do you need to take?

3. Where are you psychologically?

4. Are you excited about the prospect of fol-lowing your dream?

"Logic will get you from A to B, imagination will take you everywhere"
–Albert Einstein.

"If you don't know where you want to go, then it doesn't matter which path you take!"
–Cheshire Cat, *Alice in Wonderland* by Lewis Carrol

6

Where are you going?

"Do you know where you are going to, do you like the
things that life is showing you? Do you know?"
Diana Ross,–theme from *Mahogany.*

I was listening to a story the other day of a man who had gone scuba diving with a friend. Now as you may know, when you scuba, dive you're meant to have a buddy who stays with you. This man had somehow lost his buddy and had drifted off, going deeper and deeper into a shark infested area. Fortunately, he escaped without harm and lived to tell the tale. Nevertheless, the moral of the story is that it is so easy in this life to just drift and end up in a place where you are not even sure how you got there.

In December 2000, we were going out to Kenya to meet some very good friends, Gareth and Helen Collier, who we had met when doing our expedition through Africa. It was decided that we would go and meet some other friends in Tanzania and we would then climb up the highest mountain in Africa, Mount Kilimanjaro. Not wanting to do it the easy way, it was concluded that the five of us would hike up the lesser known route of the Western Breach Trail, called the Londrossi or Shira route. We decided to hire a guide and porters. It was a six-day hike to the top of Kilimanjaro and the top stands at 19,340 feet (5,895 m). Now, walking at altitude is difficult due to the lack of oxygen, and above 10,000 feet (3,048 m), you can start to get altitude sickness, and most people start to get headaches. Coughs and sore throats start due to the dry air, so you often don't sleep well at night either, your energy is drained and everything becomes hard work.

For the last section to the summit, you start at midnight with the idea being that you get there for sunrise. Even though we were nearly on the equator, we were above the snow line and it was very cold. At midnight, we set off expectantly behind our guide with our head torches on. After several hours of walking uphill, Jonathan and Gareth started to get worried, we didn't seem to be heading for the part of the mountain that had the breach, and we could see the head torches from other groups off in the distance having gone in a different direc-tion. Our guide had taken us the wrong way and obviously didn't know where he was going. Then came the big decision: did we try and traverse the three icy gullies to attempt to reach the other path or did we go all the way down and start again? I was already feeling exhausted and a little disorientated at this point (and if I am being totally honest, because of the dark I didn't fully comprehend the seriousness of the situation). It was icy and none of us had crampons on our feet, but we did have ski-pole type sticks. We decided to traverse. Thankfully, our friend Gareth was an outdoor instructor. I remember at one point it was still dark and even though I was standing still trying to get my breath, my feet started to slip backward. It was extremely scary. I had heard that predators can smell fear on people. I now know this to be true as I could smell fear on myself. Even though it was freezing cold, I was sweating and my sweat smelt foul. At one point, Gareth was facing me a couple of feet away and pointing with his stick saying, "Put your foot there, put your next foot there." This carried on for what felt like hours. We eventually made it across to the right path, but we still had half the height to climb. I was drained, the walk and the fear had exhausted me. It was getting light and we were still a long way from the top. What Jonathan hadn't told me about this route (or you could say that I hadn't bothered to research) was that there was a lot of scrambling (climbing using hands and feet) to get over the breach, which took even more energy. I remember

Jonathan standing behind me just telling me, "Don't turn around and don't look down." He knew I was scared of heights.

After the breach, I was totally exhausted and it still wasn't the top. My aim became to walk ten steps before stopping to have a breather, but sometimes I only got to five before I had to stop. There was a tune that would go around in my head which would build up and I would start to move my hands and sticks to it until it would get to the crescendo when I would make my feet move too. Eventually, I got to the summit where the others were waiting for me. That day, we ended up in a very dangerous situation and were walking for over thirteen hours, just because our guide didn't know where he was going.

As the above Alice in Wonderland quote says, if you don't know where you are going, it doesn't matter which path you take, but obviously the converse is true as well: if you do know where you want to go, it does matter which path you take. Just like in the illustration, you don't want to get into a treacherous situation because you went the wrong way. This is why it is so important to define your dream/ goal. You need to decide where your end point is; and it helps a lot if you can define what success looks like. I mention in another chapter about a course I have just taken which helps you win stages to speak on (something in the future I'd like to do). They ask you to determine your B.H.A.G (Big, Hairy (as in scary), Audacious, Goal) which I believe is a Zig Ziglar term. Like any 'SMART' goal, it has to be Specific, Measurable, Achievable, Realistic and Timely, i.e. it can't just be like the old Coke advert, "I'd like to teach the world to sing, in perfect harmony" as first, it's not very realistic and second, how do you know when you've achieved it?

For example, my BHAG is, "I want to help 10,000 people in the next five years to set out to achieve their own dream goals," and I will do that by writing this book, encouraging people from the stage and by creating an online course with coaching, supported by three-day retreats at the chateau where I can interact with people. My time will start once I've left full-time engineering work in Kuwait (expected to be June 2020).

This is the time to do a roadmap. As a normal road atlas will tell you how to get from A to B via C and D (i.e. London to Manchester via Birmingham), so your personal road map starts where you are, finishes where you want to be (to achieve your BHAG) and will take you on the route to get there. E.g. for me, I need to finish this book and get it published. I need to take a course to learn how to create an interesting online program, and then I need to actually create the program and build a website so that I can obtain feedback on the book and course to see how many people I help. Then I need to promote the course by speaking to audiences to share the great news about the book and course. Do you see the logical progression? I have included my road map as Appendix 4 to help you. The more you can define your map, by adding timings as milestone markers, the more you will be able to tell if you are keeping on track.

1. What do you want to have achieved in:
    3 months
    6 months
    1 year
    5 years

2. Review Appendix 4 and then draw your own road map for your dream goal. (You can also download this from my website www.mjspanswick.com)

"No one can make you happy until you're happy with yourself first"
— Your Positive Oasis

"Remember, when you forgive, you heal. And when you let go, you grow."
—BoomSumo.com

"Ships don't sink because of the water around them; ships sink because of the water that gets in them. Don't let what's happening around you get inside of you and weigh you down."
unknown

7

What are you taking with you?

"I've got no strings to hold me down"
– Walt Disney's *Pinocchio*, written by Leigh Harline and Ned Washington

"Ain't No Stopping Us Now"
–McFadden and Whitehead

My husband is a great walker and quite often encourages me to go along too. Many years ago, we decided to walk up Mount Kenya in Kenya, Africa, which is about 17,057 feet (5,199 m) above sea level. We were part of a fell walking group at work, and in the end, six of us set off to do this walk. We had decided to do it independently i.e. no guide or porters, so we would be carrying all of the goods that we needed for a six-day expedition on our backs. We were still fairly young and fit and did not see this as a problem, however what we had not experienced before was how altitude affects the body, it took a lot more out of us than we expected. As mentioned in Chapter 6, altitude sickness/fatigue kicks in around 10,000 feet (3,048 m) above sea level, and once we had reached that height, it was a hard slog, and we still had 7,000 feet (2,151 m) of altitude to climb! I remember seeing a sign near the top of the mountain that said that it was only 400 m before reaching Austria hut, which was the highest hut before the summit. That 400 m took me over half an hour to complete! I'm not saying that the journey was not worth it, certainly the view from the long-drop toilet at Austria Hut was magnificent and should be one that is experienced. However, it would have been so much easier without the full backpack. Since then, my husband and I have walked in the Himalayas but this time with a guide and porters and it has been so much easier. In fact, it was after Mount Kenya that I said "Never again, in the future we are going to put money back into the local community and not have to carry everything ourselves."

In the story *Pilgrims Progress* written by John Bunyon in the 1600s, Christian (the hero and pilgrim of the story) starts off on his journey in life carrying a large load on his back. Inside his backpack are all the worries of life, guilt, shame, insecurity etc. When he gets to the cross of Christ, the burden gets lifted off and he is able to go on his way unhindered.

The moral of this story is that we all have baggage. One of the biggest burdens that most people carry around is unforgiveness. Someone has hurt us and we just can't forgive them. As I heard Joyce Meyer once say, "Unforgiveness is like drinking poison, and expecting someone else to get ill." The thing is that the person who we are having a hard time forgiving is not affected by it at all, but it can eat *us* up from the inside, which can also affect us physically.

I was listening to a YouTube advert the other day, and they were saying that they had found a breakthrough to athletes' performance. What was their secret? They got the athletes to think for five minutes before their run and to forgive people, so that they ran without that burden. Apparently, it cut seconds off their times. As well of course as making them feel better.

Some other negative emotions to get rid of are: fear (which we will deal with separately in Chapter 11), worry/anxiety, guilt, shame, poor self-esteem, hate, resentment and anger, all of which sap our energy and weigh us down in our journey of life on the way to fulfilling our dreams.

By jettisoning the heavy loads, we have more energy to deal with what we need to deal with on the journey. (Also see the Chapter 23 on Decluttering your life)

I now hear the question – "But how do I do that?"

As mentioned, forgiveness is one of the big keys. (Remember: to forgive someone isn't the same as agreeing that what they did was right or even okay, it is simply the freeing of yourself from the trauma—cutting those strings that hold you down – like Pinocchio). Sometimes it's not others though that we have to forgive, but ourselves. If you feel guilt or shame, maybe you did something wrong or took a path that you really regret. Well if there is nothing that you can do to go back and make amends or if you cannot physically ask them to forgive you, then you just need to accept it, (if you believe in God, then ask for His forgiveness), then you have to *forgive yourself* and determine that you won't make the same mistake twice. Forgiveness is an act of the will, you can forgive someone even though you may still feel hurt; in fact by the act of forgiveness, you may decrease your hurt. Think of it as if someone has stabbed you with a knife. You will not be able to heal properly until the knife is removed. Forgiving someone is removing the knife so that it can't be twisted. When we leave the knife in, it can sometimes be accidently knocked by others close to us, which then causes even more pain.

To forgive someone/yourself, say out loud something like "(Name), I choose by an act of my will to forgive you for (Act)." You may have to do this lots of times before you start to feel better. Do it every time that the thought of what they did to you crops up in your mind.

Quite often, when we find a negative emotion we can trace it back to its root, things that happened during our formative years, but if you cannot, maybe it is something that has come down through the generational line; anger, and depression are a couple like that. If that is the case, what are the trigger points that set you off, can you avoid the triggers?

If it's poor self-esteem, then build yourself up by speaking the positive affirmations and scriptures found in Appendix 3 to yourself in the mirror each day until you believe them.

If you are a Christian, then ask the Holy Spirit to reveal the root to you and ask for healing. Go to the church and ask someone to pray with you.

1. Read the list of the emotions in Appendix 7, which ones resonate with how you feel?

2. What negative emotions do you need to ditch so you can travel unburdened?

3. Do you need help in getting rid of these? (If so, ask at your local church for someone to help you, many have trained counselors).

"If you want to go fast, go alone, if you want to go far, go in a group."
– African proverb

"People inspire you or they drain you – pick them wisely."
– Hans F Hanson

"Stay away from negative people, they have a problem for every solution."
– *The Law of Attraction*–Albert Einstein

"Don't cast pearls before swine,"
Jesus, Matthew 7:6.

8

Who are you taking with you?

"Abide With Me"
– Henry Francis Lyte

I left college in 1985, and although I had a degree in Mechanical Engineering, some of the experiences I'd had on the course left me feeling that I didn't want to have a career in pure engineering and as I was also interested in the commercial side, I decided to look for a job as a Procurement Engineer. I joined the engineering firm that I am still with, on the same day as my husband; we were doing different jobs but in the same department. Whilst I quite enjoyed the work, it didn't have the same amount of engineering to it as I had expected, but what was far worse was the management style of the head of the department. He was always picking on people, criticizing their work and generally being negative all the time. He was one of those people that if you were called into his office, it wasn't going to be good. It was my first experience of having a job, so I took it as the norm (especially way back then in the 1980s).

Now the company I worked for had an excellent training scheme for its engineering graduates that took them up to being Chartered Engineers. It consisted of two years of training where you did three month stays in different departments, went off to college to learn practical skills such as welding and then two further years of experience where you were expected to work on a construction site. Even though I'd joined as a Procurement Engineer, they accepted me onto the scheme, and I had the chance to see the work in other departments. I loved it, and several of the other department managers offered me places within their departments. It was only when I got back to the Procurement Department that I noticed how different it was. I looked at some of the good people there and thought, "Why don't you get out?" but the management style had been such that people had started to believe the criticism and so thought that no one else would want them. Luckily, I managed to get out, and flourished in one of the other departments.

Have you ever spent time with a friend and when you came away, you felt down and drained of energy? If you have, it's probably because they had been moaning about something, criticizing someone or just generally finding fault and being negative. When you are the person not only listening, but the one who they are finding fault with, it can be even more depressing. We all go through tough times when we are down and need to have a good friend we can share it with; no problem, but if it's every time you talk/see them that it happens, then there is a problem. We are warned to stay away from ingesting toxic chemicals, but so often we freely take on board toxic people who try to unload their baggage on to us. They go away feeling better, they have had someone to dump their toxicity on to, but we go away with a heavier step.

There are various reasons why people are like this: maybe they were criticized all their life as a child, their parents never thought them good enough, or maybe they have been hurt deeply in the past and so they think that nothing good in the future is going to happen. Or maybe they try and make themselves feel better by putting you down. One day, after coming back from Mt Kilimanjaro, Tanzania, Africa, (as told in Chapter 6). I was recounting the saga of the trip to a colleague, who turned around afterwards and said, "Well, if you managed it, I'm sure I would be able to do it as well," which I thought was a very strange response as there was no doubt in my mind that he was a very capable hiker, who would have been able to have done it (and probably easier than I did). However, it was after this that I noticed that he had a technique of comparing himself favourably to what others did fairly commonly and I realized that the very confident person that he portrayed was in fact a mask, and inside he was actually very insecure.

So how do you get out of toxic situations like this, because you can be certain that they are not going to help/encourage you with achieving your dream, as this will only make them feel worse about their own lives? The easy answer is to not be their friend anymore, move away, but especially if they are family, this is a lot harder to do than say. Even if you have to keep spending time with them, if you know that they are going to be negative about what your dream is, then simply don't share it with them, you are not obligated to tell everyone everything. At the very least, don't tell them until you are some way down the road to completion. Jesus tells his followers in Matthew 7:6 not to throw their pearls before swine otherwise they will trample them underfoot – and likewise, don't let negative people trample on your dreams.

So, who should you tell/take with you? Where I would start is with someone who genuinely believed in me. This could be a spouse or a family member or just a good friend, an encourager.

Another person would be a mentor; this could possibly be a life coach or depending on what you're your dream is, you can find a local expert to help you such as a teacher at a local college. (You will be surprised how willing people are to share with you their experiences if you are willing to listen and learn). Or is there a local club you can join which may have positive influencers such as the Rotary Club, which will have business people, if you want to start a business?

Another good person is a peer, someone who like you has the same or similar dream. Maybe you can find a Facebook group that you can join where people who are going through a similar situation to you can help, e.g. Entrepreneur.

In Chapter 28 I mention about a course I did where there is a Facebook group for all the people in the course (and now graduates/alumni) and except for the particular incident in Chapter 28, this has been a great source of encouragement for me, and a practical help as others ask/answer questions for one another, basically a self-help group.

1. Who has a negative influence on your life?

2. How can you stop them influencing you?

3. Who has a positive influence on your life?

4. Who will be your:

    a. Encourager
    b. Mentor
    c. Peer

"A good idea becomes a great idea, when you let it out."
unknown

"I saw an angel in the marble and carved until I set him free."
– Michelangelo

9

When are you most creative?

"I Believe I Can Fly"
–R Kelley

We all know some people who are wide awake first thing in the morning as soon as the alarm goes off, that's if they even need one, sometimes it's just the first rays of sunshine glinting over the horizon that will get them bouncing out of bed. We also know those who are night owls and may just be going out at night when the rest of us are thinking of going to bed.

Unfortunately, I found out after we were married that my husband was a lark and I was more of an owl. Except he wasn't going to accept that, and if I stayed in bed longer than 8 a.m. on a weekend, he would come in and grab the bedcovers off me, telling me to wake up as the day was almost over. I can tell you that he was on the receiving end of a few choice words when he started to do this. However, I eventually did start to appreciate the joys of the early morning. Having said that, I still don't think that it is my most creative time, or when I feel most alive which is actually the afternoon/early evening.

Whatever time it is, it doesn't really matter, but what you should do is try to use that time the most productively, i.e. if you have a difficult task to do, then do it at this time when your brain is at peak performance.

Of course, the difficulty occurs when you are also trying to do/plan your dream whilst still working full time and your most creative time happens to be when you should be at work. Whilst I would not phrase it to your boss that you would like to have your most creative/peak performance time for yourself, it may be worth at least asking if there was any way that they could be flexible with your hours so that you could come in late or go home early or have an extended lunch break to suit you. Whilst I realize that all jobs cannot be flexible, you will never know if you don't ask.

1. When in the day do you feel most creative/ most alive?

2. How can you free up that time to work on your dream goal?

"You can't use up creativity. The more you use, the more you have."
- Oscar Wilde

"Inhale possibility, exhale creativity."
- Laura Jaworski

10

Where are you most creative?

"Halfway down the stairs is a stair where I sit, there isn't any other stair quite like it! I'm not at the bottom, I'm not at the top. So, this is the stair where I always stop!"
Robin the Frog, *The Muppets*–"Halfway Down the Stairs" –A.A. Milne

This may seem like a strange heading, especially after yesterday's title of "When are you most creative?" The thing is that just as each one of us may be creative/productive at a different time of day, sometimes putting ourselves in a certain environment will help us be more creative/productive.

For example, I was working on this book when my husband and I were working in Kuwait. I had a demanding job as a PMC Project Director for a refinery worth fourteen billion dollars. I was working six days a week as standard, so my one day off a week was very precious to me. One particular day off I had put aside to work on this book, my husband wanted to go out for a run and a walk. I reluctantly agreed, feeling that I could have used the time more productively if I'd been working on the book, but then found that as we were running along (not being able to talk as we were not very fit) that all sorts of ideas popped into my head – the only problem was remembering them all when I got back. So, as well as making my husband happy, I had helped myself as well.

For some people, their most creative times are in the shower (or as per Archimedes, in the bath). For others, it's when they are walking in the country-side. And for others, it may be sitting by themselves in the study.

To work at my most productive, I need a clean desk and silence, but I know that others would prefer music/ noise around them. I can work with a messy desk though if it's only routine work to be done. Psychologically, it's good to have a set place for when you need to work, and if you do have to do it in your bedroom, choose a chair to sit in rather than the bed. If you keep a consis-tent place, then it's as if your brain thinks, "Ok, we're here now, I know what I have to do here."

Once you've had your creative moments, you will need to consolidate these by writing them up. It helps if you can have a small notepad (or smart phone) always with you, so wherever you are, you can jot some notes for later.

One place I am never creative though is when I am sitting in front of the TV, far too many distractions. What I can do in front of the TV though is type up the notes I've written earlier, so I can then get some work done whilst at least seeming to be sociable at the same time. The other place I would not recommend is lying on your bed, it's far too easy to take a snooze.

1. Where do you do most of your creative thinking/productive work?

2. What atmosphere do you work best in?

    a. Silence or noise
    b. Daylight/windows or artificial light.

3. Where were you when you first thought of your dream?

"One day you'll look back and realize that you worried too much about things that don't really matter."
– BoomSumo.com

"Stop being afraid of what could go wrong and start getting excited about what could go right!"
–Invisible Lioness

11

No fear!

"Regrets, I've had a few But then again, too few to mention."
"My Way"–Frank Sinatra

When a person knows that they are going to die, they often reflect on their life. For most people, when they look at their regrets, they find that they are due to things that they have not done or missed opportunities, rather than the things they have done, even when they messed up doing them.

I remember when I was at grammar school, about twelve years old, there was a national competition for school children to write a new Christmas carol. To make it easier, you were to take the tune from an existing carol of your choice and then put new lyrics to it. I worked hard on it and showed it to my friend, Judith. She really liked it, but when I got to the point of submission, I bottled out, thinking it wasn't good enough. Judith, however, still submitted hers. Time passed and the results came out, Judith had won an award and her prize was to travel to London and spend the day with a popular celebrity at that time (Keith Chegwin, of Tiswas, and Swapshop fame). When she heard this, she turned to me and said, "You should have submitted yours as well – it was as good as mine, and we could have gone down together!" I really regretted not having submitting it, after all, I'd done all the work, I especially regretted it afterwards when she was telling me what fun she had in London, as I had never been. But it was a fear of failure that had stopped me.

There are lots of different fears that will stop you from achieving your dream: fear of change, fear of failure, fear of what others will think, fear of wasting money, fear of looking foolish. But there is also another fear which people don't often realize: a fear of success or as some people call it "imposter syndrome." This sounds strange, who wouldn't want to be successful, isn't this what we all desire? But this fear is more subtle and it's due to our own insecurities. You feel like you are a fraud, that you don't deserve success. And if you do become successful, you will get noticed by others who will be able to see through you and know that you don't really deserve it and then it will all come crashing down and therefore, this fear makes you sabotage your venture, so that you won't have to go through that humiliating experience.

Fear is an instinct that we all have, and in its most basic form is good as it is meant to stop us from putting ourselves in danger, not standing too close to a cliff edge or not going up to a lion and patting it on its head. But fear can totally paralyze people's lives as they become more and more bound by it, as in agoraphobia where people become too scared to leave their house, making them lonely and isolated.

Nowadays, fear has become very sophisticated and subtle, your fears are more likely to be concerning what other people will think about you if your dream fails. Take heart, because from experience I have found that most people will think that at least you were brave enough to try, and will respect you for that, because so often they haven't been brave enough to chase their dream.

How many times have you worried about something that was coming up, where you have played it over and over in your mind, only to find that it turned out so much better than you feared? In fact, isn't that so often the case?

So how do you get over fear? The first thing to realize is that fear can only control you to the extent that you let it. If you are doing something new, then expect to be afraid. We are all the same, we all like to stay in our own little comfort zones and not be scared, but in real life, we just have to take a deep breath and do it anyway. Let's face it, if you let the fear of failure stop you, like I did with the carol competition, you feel a failure anyway for not trying, so you may as well give it a go, as you have nothing to lose. You cannot win if you don't enter.

The next thing is to do the thing that you are fearful of. Where fear has a big hold on you, then to conquer it may mean taking small steps to begin with. I remember when I was in my 20s, I'd been sent on a site assignment and we were building a new unit in a refinery in Belgium. My supervisor wanted me to climb to the top of a process tower up monkey ladders. I told him that I was scared of heights and whilst he understood, he wasn't going to let me get away with it that easily, "Well, you will have to learn!" The first time we tried, I only managed to climb to the first platform and even stopping there was frightening as the platform was made of steel grating that you could see through to the ground below. I held on very tightly to the handrail. He wanted me to carry on going up but I couldn't, we went back down. He then made it a regular activity and, as I pushed myself to go a little higher each time, I eventually made it to the top. I was so pleased. As I kept climbing the towers during my assignment, it got easier and easier and by the end, I was climbing them in conditions where the tower was swaying in the wind.

We often spend a lot of time imagining ourselves with horrible things happening. But switch it around and use your imagination to help you rather than hinder you; visualize yourself succeeding and everyone applauding you.

If your fear is of failure rather than of physical harm, then I suggest that you start by asking yourself some questions and actually writing the answers down. In this case, I have also included some possible answers, but answer it for yourself.

Remember, fear can rob you of your peace, your joy, your time and your destiny, *don't let it.*

The opposite of fear is courage, but courage isn't doing something without fear, it's having the fear and still doing it. Be courageous.

1. What is the very worst thing that will happen if you try and fail?

    a. People will laugh at me/think badly of me. But will they really? Why would they? I have found that most admire you for your bravery. If your friends are the sort that would revel in your failure, then maybe you need some new friends. (See Chapter 3 – Who are you taking with you?)

    b. I will get into a lot of debt. Assess what you really need to spend to start out, e.g. rent premises rather than buy or work from home. Buy second-hand equipment. Start small and build up as your business grows.

    c. What do you think will be the worst thing that can realistically happen?

2. How will you/your life be changed if it does succeed?

   a. Greater confidence in your abilities

   b. Possible income stream

   c. Will be doing something you love

   d. Will have grown in the process (overcome fear/ learnt new skills/ met new people)

   e. May get to know your purpose in this life.

   f. Your thoughts?

3. Will the world be different by you chasing your dream? How does it affect others?

   a. Employing others

   b. Providing a service to others

   c. Something else beneficial

"All things are possible to them that believe."
Jesus, Mark 9:23

"Never stop trying, never stop believing. Never give up. Your day will come"
unknown

"Sometimes life is about the ability to believe in where you are going, even when you're not sure what lies ahead."
– Venspired.com

12

Stand tall and believe in yourself!

"I'm a believer"
– The Monkees

When some animals are disturbed/spooked, they enlarge themselves, trying to make themselves seem more intimidating to the perceived threat, so that the threat will back off. Puffer fish are very good at this for example, and they blow themselves up to several times their size.

Humans do it too, if you are going for an interview, you dress up for it in a nice suit (well you did in my day), you are told to stride in with your shoulders back and your head held high and with a smile on your face. Inside you may be feeling like a shrinking violet, but as you act confidently, it actually gives you more confidence. Amy Cuddy recommends doing what is called the "Power Pose" (or Wonder Woman pose) for two minutes; before you do anything difficult, you stand up with your legs astride and arms akimbo, which raises testosterone levels, reduces cortisone and thereby reduces stress levels and allows you to think more abstractly.

The point is that by acting confidently, it can actually make you feel more confident, thereby making you a more confident person.

The thing is that if *you* don't believe that you can do something, then you are going to find it difficult to convince others that you can do it. Henry Ford said, "Whether you think you can or whether you think you can't, you're right!"

When I first started work, I was not confident at all in myself or my abilities. I hated the time of annual appraisals where you had to mark yourself as to how you had done, and I always marked myself low hoping that my boss would mark me higher. He often did, but it didn't take many years to work out that the guys who had put themselves higher generally got higher marks (and so better pay increases) even though I would have rated their work inferior to mine. I came to the conclusion that if you don't have confidence in yourself, then others won't have confidence in you either.

So, what do you do if you are not naturally confident in yourself? Well start by saying to yourself the Affirming Words or Affirming Scriptures found in Appendices 3a and 3b.

The other thing is to, "Fake it till you make it," as Lance Wallnau would say. Act as if you are already the person that you want to become (unless of course you want to become a brain surgeon!). If it's more than confidence that you need, then you should be getting the necessary education so that you do *make it* at some point.

I once went to a conference where both Annabel and Lance Wallnau were speaking. In Annabel's portion, we had to write down the answers to various questions. One of the questions was for us to name our five best friends. After we had done that, she asked us to put our hands up if our *own* names were on that list. No one put their hand up (or very few) and most of us were stunned at the question. Her point was simple. Most of us are our own worst critics, but what we need to be is our own best friend who will encourage us and believe in us. Of all the people who talk to us each day, we talk to ourselves the most, so if the voices inside your head are condemning you and telling you that it's not going to work, etc., then when you hear and recognize that, you need to "take every thought captive," i.e. say out loud, "I'm not going to listen to you anymore," and then proceed to say over yourself some of the affirming words from Appendix 3.

1. Are you on your own best friend list? If not, then make the change to put yourself there.

2. On a scale of one to ten, where would you rate your confidence in yourself?

3. If you are six or below, what method(s) are you going to use to improve it?

The Lord looked at him and said, "Go in this your strength and deliver Israel from the hand of Midian. Have I not sent you?" He (Gideon) said to Him, "O Lord, how shall I deliver Israel? Behold, my family is the least in Manasseh, and I am the youngest in my father's house"
Judges 6:14-15.

"Be yourself, everyone else is already taken."
-Oscar Wilde

"Comparison is the thief of joy."
-Theodore Roosevelt

"Stop comparing yourself to other people. You are supposed to be unique."
-Sonya Parker

"Stop comparing your life. Start living it."
-Becoming Minimalist

13

Comparison – Don't do it!

"Anything you can do, I can do better, I can do anything better than you!"
Annie Get Your Gun–Irving Berlin

Unfortunately, in this world, peer pressure is a big thing. Everyone wants to be top dog, and some people will do anything to get there. And with the social media we have today, it's too easy to compare ourselves to others and it is causing major anxiety and depression amongst teenagers because they don't think that they are good enough. The thing is though that what people are comparing themselves against is a false reality. Let's face it, we only post the photos to social media that we look nice in, or when doing exciting things. But when you are an observer, you think, "Wow they look great/they are always happy/they have so much fun..." and then you look at your own life and think, "Their lives look so much better than mine." It's only when you actually get inside their heads that you realize that they don't feel that way about themselves at all. Many years ago, when I was in college, I knew one girl who was the life and soul of everything social. I'd never known anyone who had so many friends. She was so popular. Everyone thought she was wonderful, and so confident, but when I got to know her better I found that the reason why she was so social was because she didn't actually like herself and so wanted to fill her time with other people in order that she didn't have to be with her own thoughts.

We all have our own insecurities, worries and anxieties but you can't tell that by looking at someone's Instagram post. Whilst writing this book, I was also doing an internet course about expanding your reach (about winning and speaking on stages). Everyone seemed so confident (and also so far advanced in reaching their goal), many already had their own businesses that were thriving and were being asked to speak to large audiences about what they could do for them. When I read all the posts, I got overwhelmed, then those nasty little thoughts started to creep in like, "See, you haven't even got a product to sell, why are you even on this course? Look at them, there are so many better people out there already doing similar things to what you want to do, you don't have a chance in succeeding. Why would anyone listen to you when they can go to them?"

Does this sound familiar to you?

It was then that I had to stop and think:

> Do I believe that this is what I am meant to be doing? – Yes

> Will I enjoy the process of what I'm doing? – Yes (hopefully)

If those two answers are 'Yes' – then go for it! It doesn't matter that others have done something similar to you because they won't have done it the same way that you have. They can't have because they are not you and YOU have a unique story to tell, one woven with your own experiences and insights. Your story and goal are just as valuable as anyone else's.

So, if you normally compare yourself to others, here are a few tips on how to stop.

1. Remind yourself that you are unique, you are not meant to be the same as anyone else.

2. Remind yourself of all the things that you can do and are good at.

3. Remember, life is not a competition, you may not even have the same goal as the person you are comparing yourself to.

4.   Life is big enough for *everyone* to have their own destiny and for *everyone* to succeed.

When I was going through a phase of wondering whether writing this book was right, as there must be similar products by various gurus out there already (I assumed), God reminded me that even in the Bible, there were four gospels, all similar yet unique, because the same stories had been written by different people who saw it from a different angle, and that all four gospels were meant to be there.

1.   Do you believe that your dream is what you are meant to be doing?

2.   What do you think you will enjoy during the process of following your dream?

"Success doesn't come from what you do occasionally. It comes from what you do consistently."
– Marie Forleo

"Success is nothing more than a few simple disciplines, practiced every day."
– Jim Rohn

14

Success breeds success

"Simply the Best"
– Tina Turner

H ave you ever noticed that some people are just successful; it's as if they can place their hands on anything and it succeeds, as if they have the Midas touch. In one way it's true; these people stepped out, trying something, becoming successful at it and giving them the confidence to try something else. Each time it's like a stepping stone to bigger and better things, an ever-expanding spiral.

I remember when I was promoted to Project Director, I was amazed the client had accepted me to the role, and within the first couple of weeks, I had to give a presentation to the CEO of the national organization. I was really nervous. My slides were vetted by my client and his boss. I had tried to make the presentation as comprehensive as possible, but I hadn't grasped the fact that with upper management, less is more. The presentation went well and the following week, I had to make the same presentation to the board. The same week, I also had to give a different presentation to the CEO of the parent company. After that first month as Project Director, I could have confidently presented to anyone. Learning what information to leave out was as important as learning what information to put in. But with each presentation given, I grew in confidence and soon realized that I was not only able to do the role, but to do it well.

Success then opens the doors of opportunity; people see you, notice that you are doing well and then want you on their team, whether it's the same as what you are doing now or not. A lot of the skills we use in everyday life are transferable to other situations. For example, good old common sense (which I actually don't think is that common nowadays) will go a long way in lots of different situations. Let's face it, if I had not been successful at work and in achieving my dreams, I wouldn't be here writing this book. I've never written a book before in my life, but the success I have had in other areas has given me the confidence to give it a go.

I guess right now, there are a few people reading this who will be thinking, "Well, it's all right for you to say that, but how do I get to the point of success where the expanding spiral starts?" The answer is simple: start small, just as the spiral does; the circles are tightly concentric before they expand. When you start out on any new experience, plan for success. Give yourself a bit of slack and make the target attainable.

One of the things I am very proud to have achieved is that my husband and I have run a half marathon. The gauntlet was thrown down to me the very day I had run my first ever kilometer on a treadmill. I was so chuffed at managing to run one km (0.6 miles), even though it wasn't even a mile. For me, it was a real achievement. The gym attendant listened to my achievement (done in the first week of December) and said that he would put me in for the half marathon (just over twenty-one km/thirteen miles) in the first week in March. I laughed and said, "Yeah, sure," but he was serious, and said that he would do a training schedule for me and if I followed it, I would be able to do it. I thought it impossible, and so took him up on the challenge just so I could prove him wrong. To give it a fair shot, I religiously did the training. My milestone was to be able to run three miles by the New Year and then there were several weeks of staying at three miles but doing it three times per week. My next target then moved up to running five miles, but what it wasn't, was a big jump from one mile to seven miles in one go. In the end, I had to admit that he had been right and I was wrong, but I had also won as I had managed to run a half marathon.

1. Think about your goal and plot out a few things in the preparation that could be counted as a success for you to put under your belt.

2. Give yourself a realistic timeline to achieve it.

"If you want something done, then ask a busy person!"
unknown

"I'm late, I'm late, I'm late, for a very important date, no time to say Hello –Good bye, I'm late, I'm late, I'm late."
White Rabbit, *Alice in Wonderland*, Lewis Carroll

"Being busy means that you are doing stuff. Being productive means that you are getting stuff done."
-Lifeisaboutthehustle.com

15

Time management

"Minute Waltz"
– Chopin

"If I Could Turn Back Time"
– Cher

As mentioned previously, I am currently working as a Project Director on a strategic refinery project in Kuwait (TIC $14 billion), and in this role, I often get asked to make presentations to the deputy CEO and CEO of the national company often at very short notice. If I'm lucky, I may get a day or so, but if not, I may simply receive a couple of hours' notice. However, one day I asked one of my managers to take on some extra work, he hadn't seemed very busy and this was a short-term task. Anyway, when I asked him, he said that he couldn't possibly do it because he had a workshop to organize. I was a little puzzled as I couldn't think of any workshop that was imminent, so I asked, "What workshop?" to which he replied, "The ABC workshop, it's in two months' time and I need to write the presentation!" Hmm, you can imagine that I wasn't very impressed.

So, the old adage about if you want something done ask a busy person does in fact seem to be true.

The other thing that is true is that whilst all our income levels may differ, we all have twenty-four hours in a day. And unfortunately, no one has yet found a way to turn back time, so if you waste it now, it's gone forever.

Now I know that all of our lives and responsibilities are different, some of you may have full-time jobs, as I do, others may be a full-time care-giver to babies or elderly parents. But I'm sure that if we honestly scrutinized our time, we would find time that we waste each day. There is before work (get up a bit earlier), travelling to and from work (especially if you commute by train, but even when driving, we can be listening to a relevant podcast). Now I am not advocating following our dreams in work time as that's unethical, but is there a lunch time that could be used? If you are in an open plan office, and can't use that time to work, what about going for a walk and getting your exercise then, so that doesn't take time later on? Are you able to work flexi-time so that you are able to free up the time when you are at your most creative?

Elon Musk, the billionaire owner of Tesla famously says that he works in fifteen-minute segments. Personally, for most things, I think that is too short, but it is interesting to think about time differently. The other day I was listening to a motivational podcast and they gave a tip which was, don't think in hours, but think in minutes. This helps you to make use of even the shortest time. I tried it and it was true, when I came out of one meeting and only had ten minutes before the next I would think, well it's not worth starting something now, but when you look at it as ten whole minutes , you think well I could start it even if I don't finish it , or sign a few papers, etc.

To-do lists were the big thing when I started working, they ensure you don't forget to do a task. But apparently now they are passé, the thing to do now is to schedule tasks into your calendar and then work on them at that time. Most smart-phones have calendars, where you can add alarms to remind you. I can see how that would work for big items, but personally, I still like the to-do list simply because I like the satisfaction of scrubbing it out afterwards. So, split your tasks into large ones, i.e. ones that will take more than an hour to complete, and small ones, and put the larger ones into your calendar, and keep a list of small ones handy so that if you get an extra ten minutes here and there, you can get them out of the way and scrub them off your list. Such as making that phone call to a supplier/paying a bill. Watch out though, it can be tempting to do all the small ones to get them out of the way (and so have that sense of achievement) rather than doing the larger tasks which are often a little harder. Don't fall for that trap, otherwise you will never find the time to do the larger tasks.

Once you have your lists of large and small tasks, you need to look at their priority. The Eisenhower Matrix helps with this by contrasting 'Important' versus 'Urgent'. See below.

The Eisenhower Matrix

IMPORTANT		
	2. Important but not **Urgent** - Decide when it should be done by, and put in calendar	1. Important & Urgent - Do Today
	4. **Not Urgent NOR Important** Delete or do in fill-in time.	3. **Urgent but not Important** Delegate to others if you can

URGENT

Each day, make a list of the 'Do Today' items, so that you don't get side-tracked on the tasks that are either easier or more enjoyable to do.

One tip I found useful in time management, is not to only look at your own time, but to look at the process time for whatever you are dealing with,. e.g. if you are doing something, which needs to go off to someone else for another step, before it comes back to you to finish it off, and you have other jobs that are solely down to you, then prioritize the ones that go off to someone else first, then whilst you are waiting for them to return, you can be doing the work that only depends on you. That way, you don't have dead time whilst waiting for it to return and also you are giving more time to the other person to do what they need to do.

Of course, one way to find time is to delegate. Are you delegating what you can to others, or are you the one that everyone else will get to do their work for them because they know you will? If you are a per-fectionist, then it's often difficult to delegate because you don't believe that the other person will do it as well as you can. Now there may be truth in that, but if you delegate to them and they get eighty percent of it right, then you will only have to spend twenty percent of your time on it, rather than 100%. Also, if you are a people pleaser, you may need to learn how to say 'No' occasionally, when people ask you to do something for them. If they truly love you (rather than are using you) they will understand, and believe me, saying "No" may seem a daunting task at first, but it does get easier as you keep doing it.

I've always loved reading quotes, and one of the adages I've always believed is, "Where there's a will, there's a way." In other words, if you want something badly enough, you will make it happen. And I believe that time is like that. If you really want to do something then you will make time for it, you give it *priority time*. So, what is it that you are giving priority time to at the moment?

If there were an emergency at the house, then you would make time to get it fixed, because that's a priority. So, when you have a dream, make it a priority so you will make time for it.

However, when you are planning out your time, do make sure that you plan in some 'you/family time' in the week, and set yourself a reward for achieving goals along the way, e.g. I'm going to work on my project three hours a day during the week, five hours on Saturday, but then I'm going to take Sunday off. Or I'm going to work on this topic until it's done, but then I'll take a several days off before I start the next module.

1. Knowing when you are at your most creative, how can you create time to work on your project then?

2. Categorize your tasks into large and small.

3. Are you giving your dream priority? If not, what are you giving priority to? And how are you going to change that around?

"Time stands still for no one."
-Steve Laurie

"If the devil cannot make us bad, he will make us busy."
-Corrie ten Boom

"You can't do big things if you are distracted by small things."
-Shalini Thakur

"You can always find a distraction if you are looking for one."
-Tom Kile

16

Distractions – Where are you spending your time?

"Let me entertain you"
Robbie Williams

Why is it that whenever I get up early, I actually end up getting to work later than when I get up at the normal time? Has this ever happened to you? I think I have plenty of time and then I look at my watch and suddenly realize that I'm late. I think it's because we have a psychological perception of time, so when we think that we have lots of time, we relax a bit more and the things we have to do take longer than normal. I have found the same thing when I've been on a project where there hasn't been an awful lot to do because of the stage it is in, the work I had always expanded to the time in the day.

I don't know about you, but I can often go on social media to wish a friend happy birthday, only to find an hour later that I am still looking at people's posts and I haven't even wished my friend happy birthday yet. I think we've all done it and it's easy to get caught this way. Or I've come in tired from work and put the TV on only to find that I was still there hours later and I wasn't even enjoying what I was watching, or (even more likely) I have just fallen asleep in front of it. This tells me, that whilst technology and TV can be valuable sources of information, and can sometimes save time, they can also be great time wasters. So often I find that I just fritter away time, which I should be doing something valuable with instead.

Recently, knowing that I don't want to give up using social media entirely, I've been wondering about ways to reduce the time it can waste for me. So, let me ask you a question. Do you actually know all the people that you are connected to on Facebook, etc.? If you have no intention of actually meeting up with them physically at some point in time, why do you keep them on your friends list? If you deleted some of your friends then you would have fewer posts to read. Another way to reduce the time wastage would be before you went on to social media, to set an alarm on your phone that would buzz after twenty or thirty minutes, to remind you that you should be now getting on with other things.

And with the TV, instead of having to be in front of the box at a certain time to watch it live, record it and then watch it at your least productive/creative time.

Recording has the added bonus that you can then skip all the adverts that make a forty-five-minute program into a one-hour program.

We also all spend time on essential things such as cleaning (mind you, some people would debate whether this is essential) or preparing meals, etc. or even exercise; all very important, but how can we attain the most time to work on our dreams? Do you know that thirty minutes of exercise, when you do it as 3 x 10 minutes uses the same number of calories? I have an app on my phone called 7, it's a 7-minute exercise app and it's great as a wake me up routine in the morning, and few people would be unable to say that they can't fit an extra seven minutes in the day. Even so, I did go through a couple of months when I let it slip, and got out of the routine, and you know what it's like with exercise, when you are doing it regularly, you can't imagine life without it, but when you do stop, it's so hard to start it again. But last week, my resolve returned, and I couldn't believe how much fitness I had lost. Which goes to show that doing those seven minutes a day does make a difference, and it can be the same with other things, if you can clear out thirty to sixty minutes a day and then use that for your dream planning, it will help you to gain momentum.

Another way to increase your time is to combine activities (multi-task, as long as they both don't need a lot of brain power, otherwise I feel multitasking doesn't work) but someone once gave me a fitness tip and that was to do twenty squats when brushing your teeth. Or listen to a motivational or training talk, or stick your affirming quotes on the mirror so that you are giving yourself a morning boost before you start your day, again listen to a podcast whilst washing up or cleaning the bathroom?

It is very true that time is money, and sometimes time is the rarer commodity. If this is the case with you then consider hiring a maid so that you don't need to do the cleaning yourself, or if you can't afford that, then ask your family to help out a bit more whilst you spend time on your project. Or if it's a joint project, then agree that you will do the chores one week and your partner the next. And of course, when it comes to meals, then make double/quadruple batches so that you can put them in the freezer and have home-cooked meals another time with no preparation. And while you are at it, shop in bulk or order your groceries on-line so that you don't need to drive there and then walk past all the calorie laden food.

If your children need to be driven to activities, can you set-up a car pool rotation with a trusted neighbor who is also going? None of these suggestions are rocket science, and it does mean that you have to be a bit more organized, but by doing so you can free up a lot of time to achieve your goal and it gets rid of the excuse that you haven't got the time.

1. How would you feel if your phone died, or you had no internet for a week?

2. How do you currently spend your time? Do an inventory and be honest.

3. How can you reduce wasted time to enable you to be more productive?

4. How much time can you free up to do your dream? Remember, make it a priority.

"A year from now, you will have wished that you started today."
– Karen Lamb

"Only put off till tomorrow what you are willing to die having left undone."
-Invisiblelioness.com

"In delay there lies no plenty."
– William Shakespeare

"...today is the tomorrow you talked about yesterday "
– Jaachynma N.E. Agu, *The Prince and the Pauper*

17

Procrastination

"Give me just a little more time..."
Chairmen of the Board

As I sit here starting to write this portion, I have found that I have done everything else but start. Having had a break from writing this book for a few weeks due to other pressing business, I'm finding it difficult to start back up. I've lost my momentum and I've definitely been procrastinating for the last hour, texting my sister back and forth. But now I realize that I have lost several hours of my time, I'm determined to get on with it, straight after I've made a coffee.

Unfortunately, with procrastination, there is nothing else you can do to overcome it except to just get on with it.

This is where a deadline helps. I wish I was one of those people who was well prepared and had all their revisions done before their exams. Unfortunately, I was the one that crammed all night the night before, procrastinating until I could do so no longer. But procrastination led to an unhealthy lifestyle and not very good exam results! It's far better to just "grab the bull by the horns" and take action.

Procrastination also brings with it its own stress, where you have the knowledge of things not done hanging over your head.

If we can understand *why* we are procrastinating, that will help us to find a solution to stop doing it. Here are some of the causes of procrastination.

Not knowing how to start or what to do, being overwhelmed by the task. This happens a lot. If that's you, then try breaking the task down into smaller pieces. E.g. if you are writing a novel, then start by drafting the basic story line, and character analysis, so that you have a frame in which to work. If you don't know the full story line, then just start with what you've got, you can always go back later and add earlier chapters if need be.

Doing the small jobs so that you get them out of the way. Well at least you are getting something done, but there are always small jobs to do, and it's not a good use of a block of time (say a couple of hours), because you need to use the blocks for the bigger jobs, you can always do the smaller jobs when you have less time.

Perfectionism – or fear of not doing it perfectly. Done is better than perfect. You can always come back and tweak it, but if you do something at least there is something to tweak.

Unpleasant task – but it will still be unpleasant whenever you end up doing it, so get it out of the way first, then you will get such a great sense of achievement, and you won't have it there to worry about. Bite the bullet.

One of the quotes I saw for procrastination was, "When there is a hill to climb, don't think that waiting will make it smaller," H. Jackson Brown. If it needs to be done, then it needs to be done, and it will still be there later, so all you have done by putting it off is make the worry/dread of that task bigger. If you get it out of the way first, you will not only get a great sense of achievement but it will also then give you confidence to keep going on the smaller tasks.

As well as the tips given above with the reasons, here are some more.

1. Look back at the earlier chapters (where and when you are the most creative) and create space both mentally and physically to do the task. Check when you are strongest mentally and schedule to do it then put in alarms on your phone to remind you.
2. Prepare for procrastination, i.e. don't give yourself any excuses, if you intend to exercise in the morning, then set your alarm at its loudest setting (so you can't ignore it) and put it on the other side of the room ,

so that you have to get out of bed to switch it off. Then get your exercise kit ready the night before so you don't have any excuses about not being able to find it.

3. Make a mental determination to start.
4. Make yourself accountable to someone by telling them when you are going to do it (and ask them to check if you have).
5. Reward yourself. Say, "Okay, once I've done that task, I'm going to reward myself with a cup of coffee, etc."

Remember, if a thief steals your money, you may get it back, but if a thief steals your time, you will never get it back, it is lost forever. Procrastination is a thief of time.

1. What is it that you have been putting off doing?

2. Based on the dialogue, why have you been procrastinating?

3. From the above tips, which will help you to start?

"Deep conversations with the right people are priceless"
unknown

"Wisdom is the reward you get for a lifetime of listening when you'd have preferred to talk"
- Doug Larson

18

Listen to others

"Listen, do you want to know a secret?"
The Beatles

Have you ever been to a party and you are talking to someone and you can tell that they are not listening to you? Or have you ever been listening to someone and you have let your mind wander onto other things? Or (perhaps the most common one) is that you are listening to someone and even finding it interesting, but you are thinking of what you are going to say in reply? This is very common, but we should listen, as not only may we learn something, but it gives the speaker respect. What I like about Jordan Peterson, the popular Canadian psychologist, is that when asked a question, he always pauses to think about it before giving the answer, which implies that he was listening to what they were saying when they were asking the question. I think the worst people for either not listening or simply ignoring what was asked are politicians who deliberately hear the question they want to answer.

Listening to others is a skill that we are losing as we speed on in the high-tech world. We find ourselves so busy that we multitask everything which sometimes means that we don't give people our full attention. I am definitely guilty of it, at work I have an open-door policy, so people can come in as they wish to speak to me, but when they do, they are not always given my full attention due to the stress of what is going on around me. But we should listen. You see, every one of us is different, each of us has had different experiences in our lives and it's possible they just may have the answer to the problem that you are having right now. Even if you don't have a problem right now, by listening to the right people it may save you from having a problem in the future. First of all, we need to be humble enough to ask for their opinion/view, and then we need to listen because that's how we learn. Even if they have not been through something exactly the same, what they say may be enough to trigger a solution for you. And as an added bonus, it may just make their day to see that they have helped you. One of my Project Managers at the moment is very experienced in not only building refineries but also in running them. He is well-respected and has a lot to offer, however he is not very forthcoming in giving his opinion. When asked about this his reply was simple, "If someone wants my opinion, then they will ask for it," with the implication that if someone asks for it then they will be ready to listen. I learnt that day to always ask. Many people are afraid to ask because they believe that they may get laughed at as it shows their ignorance, but on the contrary it shows wisdom, as you are wanting to grow/learn and gain in knowledge. You may also be very surprised to see that people are happy to be asked for their opinion and very willing to help you out.

However, as well as listening to others, remember to listen to yourself. It's really good to seek the advice of others, but at the end of the day, if you are making a decision that affects *your* life, then *you* are the one that has to be responsible for that decision. Whenever you are making a big decision then always ask your-self the question, "Do I have peace with this decision?" If the answer is "No" then it's probably best to think about it again.

1. Do you have a trusted counselor who you can bounce ideas off of, and who will give you an honest answer?

2. Schedule some time to talk to them about your dream.

"Set goals. Reach. Repeat."
-Startup Vitamins

"Q. How do you eat an elephant?
A. One mouthful at a time!"
African Proverb

19

Are we there yet? (Set realistic targets)

"Are we there yet?"
Little Baby Bum

Have you ever been on a long road trip with a child? The excitement of starting the trip soon wanes, as they become bored, tired and hungry, and just like Donkey in the film *Shrek*, the mantra soon becomes, "Are we there yet?"

If you know where you are heading, you can gauge how far you have come and how far you have to go. Sometimes we forget to stop and look back to where we have come from. It is good to periodically take stock of what you have achieved in getting to where you are. Celebrate your successes or as in the illustration above, tell the children, "When we get to place X, we will stop for an ice cream."

When you have a big goal you want to achieve, it is easy to get overwhelmed with it; it seems so big that you don't know where to start, just like eating an elephant may seem like a mammoth task (pun intended). If this is the case with you, then you need to break it up into smaller parts or as the African proverb says, "one mouthful at a time."

Sometimes when we have looked at the renovation of the chateau, it has seemed overwhelming. If you looked at every task that needed to be done, it would just seem impossible. So, we decided to be more strategic, i.e. what needed to be done to stop it deteriorating further? In our case, we started with the barn which had virtually no roof, leading to rain getting into the stonework causing it to disintegrate. So although it didn't add to the chateau itself, it was essential the barn roof was mended first to ensure the barn didn't collapse. Another essential job was to stop the dampness from getting worse in the kitchen area. In order to this, we needed to take the water away from the walls (especially as being built in the twelfth century, it didn't have any foundations), so we had to have drains put in underground. The building also didn't have a proper sewage system (again which meant digging up outside) nor water to the owner's wing (never mind any central heating).

Once we had secured the outside, we then started on the rooms inside, the oldest tower so that it could be rented out as a holiday home in the summer time.

In an attempt to stop the dampness, previous owners had tanked the walls with concrete, which unfortunately meant that the dampness stayed in the walls. The last owners had then covered up the mess with plaster board rather than sorting the problem out. As the place had been empty for two years by the time we saw it, the dampness and mould were showing through the plaster board. We hired some heavy-duty hammer drills and got stuck in, then afterwards used a breathable render together with an old-fashioned whitewash to cover it. The 'holiday let' part (the gite) was finished three years after we bought it. The owner's wing has more work to be done in the rooms, and although altogether we have now had the chateau for nine years, we still get a bit overwhelmed by how much there is still to do. However, at least now we have got to the stage where most of the structural changes have now been completed inside. It would have been very easy to get discouraged with all of the work, especially when you start one job and find three more to do. And I would be lying if I said it never got to us, but we still love the place and love seeing the transformation and one day, we will take great pleasure in boring all our friends with all the before and after photos.

Don't forget that progress in the right direction is still progress, even if it's only small. If your dream is about learning a new language or skill such as learning to play a musical instrument, then remember that a few minutes every day is better than a few hours every so often, because we are forming memory links in our brains and then reinforcing them when we repeat them, and creating good habits. Also, if you are doing something toward your goal everyday then you are keeping it in the forefront of your mind and you will be surprised how momentum will build up, giving you an impetus and enthusiasm to keep going and finish.

If you did a road map earlier, you will have put in milestones along the way of where you need to go to achieve your dream. If you haven't already done so, now is the time to add the time markers in as well, i.e. what do you need to have achieved in the first year, second year, etc.? Also, in your roadmap, don't forget to add in some easy wins, these will help you to stay encouraged as you go along.

When you are doing either your plans or even the road map, you do need to ensure that the schedules are achievable otherwise you will get discouraged, but on the other hand, we all work a little better when we are under a bit of time pressure. But if it's a long-haul job, or like us you are doing it part-time/in your holidays, then do allow times of non-pressure as well, i.e. ensure that you have a sustainable speed as in a marathon, rather than trying to sprint all the way. And when you have achieved a milestone, then remember to take time out and celebrate it before pushing for the next marker.

1. Is your dream going to be one of marathon proportions or a sprint?

2. If you haven't done so already then complete your road map (see Appendix 4 or www.mjspanswick.com) and fill in the timescales. (Don't forget the easy wins.)

"Don't race for the finish line – Enjoy the journey."
-Averstu.com

"In between goals is a thing called life, that has to be lived and enjoyed."
-Sid Ceasar

"Look around you. Appreciate what you see. Nothing will be the same in a year."
unknown

20

Enjoy the ride

"Three wheels on my wagon, and I'm just rolling along"
The New Christy Minstrels

I remember one time when we were driving through Africa, we had just crossed the border into Ethiopia and we wanted to go down to the Elmo Valley to see the Mursi Tribes people there who have the large disks in their lips. We set off early in the morning, but as the day went on, the roads got worse and worse, and we ended up driving down a dried-up river bed. This of course is something that you're not meant to do, due to flash floods, but the road had just petered out and this was the only option. We drove along for hours; it was getting later and later, and I was thinking that we should have arrived there by now. We tried to get out of the river bed but as we were driving up the bank, something went crunch, we carried on and then as we were going along, there was another crunch and the car just stopped. In the guidebook it had said that, "Whatever you do, do not wild camp in this area because there are many bandits around who will rob you." But we had no choice but to stay there. It was getting dark and the engine mountings had all failed. I was terrified and I spent most of the night awake just praying for safety and a solution. In the morning, my prayers were answered as my husband, who is exceedingly practical, managed to fix up the engine mounts using pieces of wood and rope. We limped along only managing to travel at walking pace, so that we did not break the fix, and that day we saw twelve new species of birds that we would never have noticed before, had we not broken down and had to limp along. The thing is, that once we had accepted the fact that we had to go at that speed, there was no point getting frustrated, we had to make the most of it. Going faster than we did, may have meant breaking down again and as with anything, slow progress in the right direction is better than no progress at all.

If you are doing your dream just because you think it will make you money, then you are probably doing it for the wrong reason and you may lose interest when things take time or get tough. However, if what you are doing is your passion, then you are able to enjoy the process, knowing that you are working toward your goal.

We've also experienced this with the Chateau. We've been working on the owner's wing portion for approximately six years and there is still a long way to go. It's slow because we are just working on it in our holidays (and periodically taking a holiday elsewhere as well). But whilst we wanted to finish the holiday-let part as soon as possible so that we could rent it out and earn some money, with the owner's wing we decided we were going to take our time and get the feel for the place before we made any design changes. We therefore didn't set a high schedule expectation only to be disappointed. We know it will only get finished once we are living there on a full-time basis.

1. Are you enjoying what you are doing to get to the place you want to be?

2. Is the journey/process part of your dream, or just a means to an end?

"By failing to prepare, you are preparing to fail."-
Benjamin Franklin

*"Give me six hours to chop down a tree and I will spend the
first four sharpening the axe."*
-Abraham Lincoln

"Success occurs when opportunity meets preparation."
unknown

"Proper preparation prevents poor performance."
-Charlie Batch

21

Preparation and planning

"One day at a time."
Marijohn Wilkin/Kris Kristofferson

Whatever your dream may be, it's always best to do a bit of homework before you set out. In Chapter 22, I go into "Counting the cost" but you can only do that if you know what you are letting yourself in for.

If you haven't already done so, I suggest you complete the Dream Questionnaire in Appendix 1. If you are right at the beginning of your journey, this will help you clarify what you need to do.

Obviously how much planning you need to do depends on what your dream is and how big your goal is.

One of the dreams that Jon and I have fulfilled was to drive from the southernmost tip of Africa (Cape Agulhas) back to the UK. It originally started as London to Cape Town, but I'll go through that story another day. We were preparing for the trip for nearly three years, but the time wasn't just for planning, but also the saving up to be able to afford it. Part of the time was spent buying and preparing the vehicle. Jon loves Land Rovers and is a very good amateur mechanic. For the journey through Africa, we needed to add an extra fuel tank, a water tank, heavier coil springs, guards for the underside, roof rack, off road tires etc. We obviously had to decide which countries we wanted to visit. Had to check the safety alerts (when we did the trip, the Sudanese borders were closed, so we had to go Ethiopia, Eritrea then by ship to Saudi Arabia). We also had to get the Carnet (vehicle passport/insurance) so that we didn't have to pay import/export charges every time we crossed a new border. Then there were the medical aspects, what vaccines would we need? What medicines should we take with us? This is all besides where did we want to visit in each country and where would we stay. In order to reduce the cost, we invited two friends to come with us. Then we split the list of the countries that we intended travelling through between us so that there was less research to do, although each of us could look at the others countries as well if we wanted to. As Sue was a Planning Engineer by profession, she also scheduled where we should be at what time in order to miss the rainy seasons in each country (in theory).

For the other dreams that we undertook, we didn't do quite as much planning, due to the fact that we were not giving up paid employment to do them, the execution timing was not as critical, neither were the consequences if we didn't do it.

So how much preparation and planning you need to do depends on how critical the consequences of not doing it are. If you are giving up work to follow your dream, it's best that everything is in order before you resign so that it takes less time to get up and running without income. If you are not giving up work, then it might not be so critical. Certainly, with the trip to Africa, if we hadn't gotten everything in order before we went, such as the carnet, we would have been stuck owing thousands and thousands of pounds at each border crossing in import and export duties for the Land Rover, which would have jeopardized the trip. Also going to lectures concerning medical issues also helped when we were in the middle of the bush. Even though I took prophylactics for malaria, and covered up every evening, I still managed to catch malaria. The doctor that diagnosed it though prescribed the wrong drug to cure it. From the lecture, I knew what the matching drug to cure the malaria was, as they had told us the pairing with the type of prophylactic that we had been using. And as we had made sure to include some of this in our medical kit, all I had to do was take it and then wait out the three days of fever.

Now when we talk about planning, there are actually two aspects to this, one is knowing what you have to do and the second is putting those items into a schedule/Gantt Chart.

You may be thinking, well I don't know how to do that, but in reality, I bet everyone has done some planning at one point or another and I'll give you two examples of that.

Example One–Planning a Holiday

The first thing you need to do is decide when and where you want to go. Ensure that the people that you want to go with can also make that week. If you are working then you/they may need to check that you/they will be able to get the time off and that colleagues are available to cover.

You also need to know your budget. Then you can research the details of which hotel, etc. Then you need to decide how you are going to get there and book flights if necessary.

You will also need to check if you have a valid passport and investigate whether or not you need to obtain a visa, vaccinations and travel insurance. Then of course just before you go, you will need to pack and get currency.

But you may not have thought of this as planning as you do it subconsciously.

Example Two - Organizing a Wedding

The other example I was going to use which people do recognize as needing a lot of planning is the organizing of a wedding. If you've either organized one or helped someone else you will know that it's best to start one to two years in advance of the wedding date, especially if you want it in summer at a specific rented venue. Not knowing this, my husband and I set a date only six months ahead and we had an awful time trying to find a photographer and reception venue. It was probably the worst planned wedding ever and if I were organizing it now, it would be done very differently.

Having a clear idea of what you want to achieve will help considerably with all your preparation.

To help, I have added in Appendix 8 a simple schedule/Gantt Chart based on my activities for this dream. Note: in some periods you may be under-taking more than one task, so it's ok to have bars which overlap, just make sure that what does overlap is rea-sonable for the time you have.

It has been created in Excel and if you want to adapt it for yourself, a copy can be found at www.mjspans-wick.com. You can find more sophisticated and specific software (some even free) on the internet, where you can track the time and the progress made, but simple is often best to start with.

1. Will you be giving up paid employment to undertake your dream?

2. How critical is the preparation phase to your dream?

3. What specific areas need planning work for your dream?

4. Have you allowed that time in your plan?

"Suppose one of you wants to build a tower. Won't you first sit down and estimate the cost to see if you have enough money to complete it? For if you lay the foundation and are not able to finish it, everyone who sees it will ridicule you, saying, 'This person began to build and wasn't able to finish.'"
Jesus, Luke 14:28-30 NIV

"Where there's no pain, there's no gain."
Fitness slogan

22

Count the cost

"Count the Cost"
David Meece

A re you someone who is impetuous, so keen that you jump into situations without thinking, or are you someone who is more meticulous and has to have all the i's dotted and the t's crossed before you will make a move?

If only we could speak French just by buying a French book/DVD/course, or lose weight by buying a diet book, life would be so much easier. But unfortunately, to succeed in life you will need to have determination, perseverance and be willing to undertake some hard work.

When I say to count the cost, I'm not just talking about money (although there is that aspect as well). When we bought the Chateau in France, it needed a lot of work. It looked a mess, had lots of dampness and the ground floors didn't even have floors, they were just earth. As Project Managers, the first thing we should have done was calculate how much it was going to cost us, but not knowing the French labor market, we took the estate agents estimates at face value (big mistake as they were very keen to sell it to us). What we found out afterwards was that we should have taken their estimate and doubled it. Thankfully, we hadn't given up our day jobs, and so still had an income stream. We also decided to start work first on the area that we would be able to rent out, so bringing further money in.

Being practical people, we were looking forward to physically working on it ourselves, and so every holiday we would go over there, put our scruffy clothes on and get stuck in. In one way it was great—lots of physical exercise and it was exhilarating seeing the transformation of the place. They say "a change is as good as a rest" but when you are going from a stressful situation at work to a physically stressful situation *continually,* it can take a toll on you. My client said to me a couple of times that I seemed to come back to work more tired after the holiday than when I went. I remember some friends saying to us, "Don't forget to enjoy yourself there as well as working, otherwise you will start to dread your time there." Unfortunately, because we don't get much time there, we have not taken the time to enjoy it as we feel under pressure to get the work done. However, they are right and we need to take time to enjoy it as well.

Basically, if you want to achieve anything in this life you can't just expect it to happen, but you need to make it happen. As the saying goes, it will take, "Blood, Sweat and Tears" to succeed (if it's a big goal anyway) and there will be times where you will get discouraged and fed up and wonder what you got yourself into it, but then of course you need to remind yourself of why you started it in the first place. Remember, if you never try anything you will never succeed at anything. This chapter isn't meant to put you off starting your dream goal, but you should go into a situation with your eyes open. By counting the cost before you begin, you need to recognize that there may be a toll on you, financially, physically, emotionally , and relationally and if you realize that now, but still think it's worth doing , then when those times come you can tell yourself, yes, I know that this is hard, but it's going to be worth it in the end. If you don't count the cost before you start, then you may be tempted to give up when you hit your first road block.

1. Remind yourself of your "Why" for undertaking your dream.

2. Write down what cost you are willing to pay to achieve your dream goal in the following categories.

   a. Financially–do you know how much money it will take?

   b. Emotionally–if it's a dream that will take time to achieve, will you have the emotional perseverance to see it through?

   c. Relationally–will you need to spend time away from your loved ones?

   d. Physically–will it be physically demanding?

3. Is achieving your dream goal worth the above demands? (It may be worth going through the same questions with the benefits of achieving your goal) i.e.

   a. Financially–Will achieving your goal bring in an income stream?

   b. Emotionally–What sense of satisfaction will you achieve with your dream?

c. Relationally—Will the achievement of your dream be beneficial to your loved ones?

d. Physically—Will you be fitter and stronger once you've achieved your goal?

"You can't reach for anything new if your hands are full of yesterday's junk."
-Louise Smith

"Clutter is no more than postponed decisions."
-Barbara Hemphill

"Letting go of physical clutter also declutters the mind and the soul."
-April Williams

"Make room for what matters – it's that simple."
-Robert Trew

23

Decluttering your life

*"Set me free why don't cha babe
Get out my life why don't cha babe
Cause you don't really love me
You Just Keep Me Hangin' On..."*
The Supremes

The chateau has ten or eleven bedrooms and it is a great joy when we go around the shops and markets and buy something that we think will really suit the place. However, as the chateau is only half restored at the moment it isn't ready to receive the beautiful goods we are buying, so it all ends up in the storage room which will one day be a lounge/sitting room. Unfortunately, this room has become so cluttered that we are not even sure what we have anymore.

We are also working on several rooms at the same time, so these have become cluttered with building equipment/scaffolds and tools. The first thing I want to do next time we go is to tidy up all of the tools and equipment. Why? Because it has become very inefficient to have to go hunting for the hammer/screwdriver/drill that you want, every time you want to use it. Put it back where it belongs and then you will know where to find it.

We talked earlier about where are you the most creative, and I think that for most people, we work best when there isn't a mess all around us. So, if you are going to start a new project (which a dream is) then unless you are a *mad professor* type, you probably will work and think best if things are orderly around you. If everything is a mess, you are more likely to get overwhelmed and discouraged. So why not spend an afternoon just decluttering the room where you are going to work. To do this, get four separate boxes/bags, one – items that you want to keep but are in the wrong place, such as the tools, two – goods to sell, three – things to take to a charity shop, four – stuff for the rubbish. And once you have filled the boxes, make it a priority to dispose of them appropriately. You may even reconsider if you want to combine boxes two and three and take them all to the charity shop, if you don't think you will get around to selling them quickly. If an object brings back negative memories, then definitely get rid of it. A lot of parents keep a lot of things that their children made for them because they have very positive memories attached. But if you need more space, why not take a photo of the painting/craft, so that you can still look back at the memory without having the clutter to go with it.

To encourage you, take a before and after photo to show what you have achieved and to encourage you in the future.

We have spoken about how to declutter your life from physical goods, but what about other things in your life? In Chapter 7 we mentioned how it's easier to travel through life with as little baggage as possible and that included emotional baggage. Have you decluttered your life of that yet?

1. Do you need to declutter your house, your emotions or both?

2. Set a time to do it, if possible, do something toward it today.

"Winners are not those who never fail, but those who never quit."
— Edwin Louis Cole

"The temptation to quit will be greatest just before you are about to succeed."
Chinese Proverb

"Some people want to see you fail – disappoint them."
Joker, *The Dark Knight*

24

No quitting

"When the going gets tough, the tough get going."
– Billy Ocean

It's not often that things at work have made me want to quit, but I do remember one instance. I had been newly promoted, and for my first project in my new position as Project Engineering Manager they sent me on assignment to Teesside in the north of England on a pharmaceutical project. Having previously worked on oil refinery projects, engineering and building a pharmaceutical manufacturing facility was completely new to me. We had an engineering office in Teesside so most of the other engineers came from there and already knew one another, but didn't know me. So here I was trying to prove myself in a new role, and a new industry to people who didn't know me at all. Coupled with that, the Project Engineer who was working for me was a couple of years older than I was and was resentful that I was now his boss. What made this even worse was that he had worked well previously with my new boss, the Project Manager, and so the Project Manager, would often go directly to the Project Engineer, missing me out of the loop. I was trying my best to learn the new role and the new industry, but it was all getting on top of me, especially without friends and family to support me. At the time Jonathan was working on assignment on the other side of the country so every weekend one of us would drive across country to see the other or we would go back to our house in Reading. Every weekend as I travelled back to Teesside I would get this feeling of dread in my stomach. This carried on for months, but the final straw came when the Process Engineers had completely ignored my instruction and had also gone against their own procedures, and gave me drawings to check at 5 p.m. before they were due to be reviewed by the client the following morning. Because they had ignored my instructions, and their own procedures, the quality of the drawings was appalling and when I told them it was all wrong, all I got was back-chat. I was fuming. That night, I went home and cried, wondering what I was doing there. I just wanted to throw in the towel. The following weekend, when I was travelling by train from Reading, I was looking out of the window, and I saw a reflection of a face that said, "If you don't give up, I will give you the victory," and then disappeared. I also felt I was meant to have a frank talk with my boss to clear the air. After that, I was determined to see the project through and I found that in the process I grew, and it made me stronger, and the project turned out a success.

I was listening to a podcast today that said that eight years before his "I have a dream" speech that Martin Luther King Jr. had written a letter to God about how discouraged he was and how he wanted to quit the cause. We don't know how God replied, but the world should be very grateful that he didn't quit.

It's easy to think that running away from a situation is the best option, but often it isn't, because whatever you run away from, often comes back another time for you to face.

If you feel like quitting, here are some suggestions.

1. Don't make any rash decisions when you are feeling angry, down or upset.

2. Get some rest. Things often seem worse when you are tired.

3. Take some time out away from the situation, go to a location where you normally feel good, like the sea or mountains, back to nature, and go for a walk to clear your head. Distract yourself to relax.

4. Take pen and paper and write down the answers to the following questions, be specific, not just one or two words.

   a. What your dream goal was.

b.   The 'why' behind your dream. (Why did you want to do it in the first place?)

c.   Have either of these changed?

d.   Write down things in life you are grateful for.

e.   Ask yourself, "What is my dream worth to me?"

5.   Look back over what you have achieved so far, in getting where you are now – both the successes and the obstacles you overcame.

6.   Review what you have invested into your dream so far, both self-investment and financial investment – Will this be lost if you quit now?

7.   Look into the future and ask your future self how they would feel if you quit now. (Have you ever given up on something previously that you later regretted?)

8.   Discuss the situation with loved ones.

9.   Seek external advice from professionals.

10. Pray (even if you are not a believer) and ask for guidance.

1. Answer and reflect on the above questions.

2. Look up the classic poem "Don't Quit" by John Greenleaf Whittier. The last verse and stanza go:

Success is failure turned inside out
The silver tint of the clouds of doubt,
And you never can tell just how close you are,
It may be near when it seems so far;
So stick to the fight when you're hardest hit—
It's when things seem worst that you must not quit.

For all the sad words of tongue and pen,
The saddest are these: "It might have been."

"Obstacles are those frightful things you see when you take your eyes off the goal."
– Henry Ford

"A champion named Goliath, who was from Gath, came out of the Philistine camp. His height was six cubits and a span.[1] He had a bronze helmet on his head and wore a coat of scale armor of bronze weighing five thousand shekels; on his legs he wore bronze greaves, and a bronze javelin was slung on his back. His spear shaft was like a weaver's rod, and its iron point weighed six hundred shekels. His shield bearer went ahead of him.

As the Philistine moved closer to attack him, David ran quickly toward the battle line to meet him. Reaching into his bag and taking out a stone, he slung it and struck the Philistine on the forehead. The stone sank into his forehead, and he fell face-down on the ground."
1 Samuel 17: 1-7 and 48-49 (Read the full story if you have time-See Appendix 5)

---

[1] This equates to about 9' 4" tall.

25

Overcoming obstacles/slaying your giant

"I Will Survive"
– Gloria Gaynor

"What doesn't kill you makes you stronger"
– Kelly Clarkson

To succeed in life you are going to have to face and overcome various obstacles. If your goal was easy to do, then many others would have already done it. Anyone who has ever succeeded in life will tell you that to get where they wanted to go, they had to fight for it at some point or another. If your goal isn't worth a fight, then why are you doing it?

Every butterfly that you have ever seen has had to fight to get out of its chrysalis. The act of breaking out is what prompts the process of the fluid being sent to the wings so they are able to unfold. Once out, they have to wait a short while, whilst their wings fully expand and dry out, and then they can fly off.

In the story above, David (later King David) was only a teenager. He wasn't part of the army but his father had sent him with some food to give to his older brothers who were. Goliath had been goading the Israelites for forty days saying that they should select a champion to fight him and that would decide the war. However, the Israelites had taken one look at him and were too afraid to fight, and who can blame them, he was over nine feet tall.

So, what made David different from all the other Israelites?

- He hadn't been worn down by the taunts of Goliath for forty days.

- The Israelites only saw the problem (Goliath) but David looked at his resources (God) to overcome the problem.

- When the problem taunted him, he spoke back to the problem (Goliath) saying that his resources were greater, thereby encouraging himself and keeping himself positive.

- He didn't try and solve the problem using the traditional method that wasn't going to work; he refused the king's armor so that he wouldn't be weighed down.

- Rather than trying to fight Goliath on his terms, i.e. at short range hand to hand combat, David attacked first using the skills that he had learnt in a different arena (slingshot).

Goliath thought that his size was his strength, but to David, Goliath's size made him a bigger target to hit. If whatever you are doing is a worthy goal, you can be sure that at some point you will come up against obstacles that will try and stop you. It takes courage (which is taking the action despite the fear) to succeed in the face of obstacles; if you don't have courage, then you will fail in most endeavors you try because there will *always* be a time when you have to overcome an obstacle or a challenge. However, if you know how to solve the problem, but you are not doing it, then your problem isn't the obstacle, but rather a fear of failure or a fear of success.

According to Rick Joiner's book *Leadership – the Power of a Creative Life*, there are four main ways that people react to problems:

The obstacle makes people turn back—people give up and fail to achieve their goal.

The obstacle stops people in their tracks. You may not have given up and retreated but you've stopped from advancing. Keeping your dreams but not moving forward in the long term will lead to frustration and most likely defeat, but everyone is allowed a breather.

The obstacle makes you change your course. This is a valid way of solving a major problem (See also Chapter 27), but if we let every little obstacle change our course then the chances of reaching your goal diminish.

Going against the obstacle head on and overcoming it. In other words, slay your giant.

When you come against obstacles with your dream, learn from the lessons of David:

- Don't let the problem intimidate you

- Keep a positive attitude about being able to overcome

- Look at what skills you already have from different areas of your life/other problems that you have solved to tackle the problem (David had previously fought a bear and a lion)

- Look to resources outside of yourself to help. Ask a mentor/someone who has been through a similar situation to help

- Pray to God to give you wisdom in the situation.

1. What problems have you overcome in the past?

2. How did you feel before and after overcoming?

3. What lessons did you learn from that problem?

4. Define your current problem–what is it you have to resolve? Once defined, can you break it down into smaller problems?

5. How can your obstacle/problem be turned into an opportunity?

"When everything seems to be going against you remember that the airplane takes off against the wind, not with it."
– Henry Ford

"If you are going through hell – keep going"
– Winston Churchill

"Hardships often prepare ordinary people for an extraordinary destiny."
– CS Lewis

"The best view comes after the hardest climb."
unknown

"Every adversity, every failure, every heartache carries with it the seed of a greater or equal benefit."
– Napoleon Hill

"When life gives you lemons, make lemonade!"
unknown

26

What to do when things go wrong

*"Joshua fought the battle at Jericho, and the walls came
tumbling down."*
African American Spiritual, Ray Roberts 1865.

S ometimes our lives just seem to come tumbling
down around us, a bit like the walls of Jericho.
The security that we thought we had just isn't there
any longer. Whether that is money in the bank or the
loved one whose support you relied on.

You may have heard the saying ,"I was taking one
day at a time, but several ganged up on me at once!"
and it can be like that in life, believe it or not, even
the rich and famous have things that go wrong in their
lives. Even if they are putting a smile on for the cam-
eras doesn't mean that they are not hurting inside,
because life is like that, no one gets off scot-free.

In the last couple of weeks, as well as trying to
write this book, my ageing mother ended up in the

hospital in the UK, my day job in Kuwait became incredibly stressful and I had meetings in Korea to attend and then my husband went into the hospital in Kuwait for a small operation and ended up in intensive care! It just felt all a bit too much when it all came in the same month.

Often, we can feel like a juggler who has many plates spinning in the air on poles, and we are desperately trying to get around to each pole to ensure that the plates don't fall off.

1. One of the things to do when things have gone wrong is to stand back and review. Stop what you are doing and take time to reflect. Ask yourself the following questions:

2. What has actually gone wrong? i.e. what is the problem?

3. Why has it gone wrong? What was the root cause of the problem?

4. Was I part of the problem (be honest)?

5. Is there anything that can be done to rectify the problem? And if so, what?

6. Is there any way that this problem can be turned around to a positive, e.g. making

lemonade? (Did you know that if a company handles a complaint well, then that can turn an unhappy customer into a very impressed one who will then praise you to others?)

7. What lessons can be learnt so that the same situation doesn't happen again?

8. If there are multiple problems that contributed, which one is the most urgent to solve, i.e. which plates can be allowed to fall from the poles?

9. Is it time to bring professional help in to deal with the problem?

10. Are there any websites/forums where you can ask others how they have dealt with similar problems?

Last year we rented out part of the chateau to paying customers. We asked the pool man to visit twice a week. Unfortunately, the pool turned green whilst the guests were there. It was a hot summer and obviously the client was upset that his children couldn't use the pool. I tried ringing the pool man, no answer, I tried texting and WhatsApp, again no answer. In the end, Jonathan flew back from Kuwait to sort it out himself.

We gave the client a discount for not being able to use the pool for a few days and he was so impressed with how Jon had dropped everything and had flown all that way to deal with the problem, that he gave us a glowing review. The lesson learnt was that we couldn't trust the pool man to respond when necessary to ensure customer satisfaction, and we will have to be there in the future to deal with the pool and anything else that may go wrong.

1. Write down the answers to the questions 1-9 written above.

"Changing direction in life is not tragic, losing passion in life is."
-Max Lucado

"Sometimes in the winds of change we find our true direction."
Toby Mac #SpeakLife

"Small steps in the right direction are better than big ones in the wrong direction."
unknown

"She wasn't where she had been, she wasn't where she was going, but she was on her way."-
Jodi Hills

27

Are you still going in the right direction?

"Show me the way to go home! I'm tired and I want to go to bed."
Irving King

Did you know that if a rocket set off from the earth to reach the moon and veered off its trajectory by only one degree, it would miss its target by 4,400 miles (7,040 km) by the time it should have landed?

Many years ago, when my husband and I worked in the UK, we were members of the works Fellwalking Club; in fact for many years, Jonathan was one of the organizers. One year, it was decided that we would do the 3-Peaks Challenge. This is normally a twenty-four-hour event, but in order to give everyone a chance to take part, we attempted it in forty-eight hours. For those of you reading this who are unaware of what it is, the aim is to walk/climb up the highest mountain in

Scotland (Ben Nevis), England (Scafell Pike) and Wales (Snowdon) within the time limit and obviously travel in between them as well. All was going well when we got to Ben Nevis, it was a nice day and it seemed a fairly easy walk, however it all started to go wrong when we were travelling down to Scafell Pike as we ended up going through the middle of Glasgow and getting terribly lost and traffic bound (this was a long time before GPS and Google Maps). This meant that we arrived at Scafell Pike several hours later than planned, added to which, the weather had turned from a nice sunny day to being quite miserable. As we started up the mountain it got colder and foggier, with visibility reducing enormously and we were all relieved when we made it to the top. We set off joyfully thinking that that was now two out of three that we had bagged but unfortunately, we started off on a clear path, but in the wrong direction. Now Jon is very good at directions and orienteering, and was often checking the bearings with map and compass, and so after a while, he got concerned that we were going the wrong way. He managed to persuade some of the other experienced walkers of this and so the only way to correct this was to slog back up to the top again (not a popular option as by now it was getting late and we were all tired). Two of the group though had gotten too far in front to be able to tell (yes, it was before cell phones were invented as well). They were experienced walkers so we were not worried about their safety. Once we reached the top for the second time, multiple readings were taken to ensure that our first mistake didn't repeat itself. We were cold, wet and tired, and we ended up being on the mountain all night, eventually reaching our accommodation at 5 a.m. After a few hours of sleep, we eventually got a phone call at the accommodation that the other two were safe, they had continued to follow the path down the wrong way and ended up in a valley on the other side of the mountain, and now wanted to be picked up by the minibus. So, after several more hours delay we made it to Snowdon which was bagged thankfully without any further events.

The point here is that it can be quite easy to be merrily going along in a certain direction, thinking that everything is fine because the path is quite broad and easy. But the question is, are you still on target to reach your goal? And if not, do you need to change your path to get back on the right track or are you happy (as the two walkers were) to continue on this path knowing that you will end up at a different destination, and you need to recalibrate your goal?

Of course, the first thing is to realize that you are actually going in the wrong direction. But how do you know?

When you are walking along following a map, you can look at the contours or landmarks shown on the map and see if they are actually around you. If they are not, then you are not where you think you are. Life has a way of giving us signposts to where we are and where we are heading, but if you are so intent on speeding along, you can sometimes miss them; whether it's in our relationships, our jobs or even our own health and wellbeing.

Take time out once in a while to assess where you are and where you are heading. e.g. if you are running a business, then are you getting the sales you need to break even? If not, why not? And what can you do to rectify it? If you don't know, then ask a small business advisor to help, or if you belong to a guild, ask someone if they would do a cold eyes review on your business to see if there was anything that you are missing. If you are in the UK, contact https://www.gov.uk/business-support-helpline or ACAS.org.uk.

Maybe your company is doing well but you are so stressed at the workload that you are yelling and screaming all the time at your workers. Are your workers/family stressed out due to the pressure you are putting them under?

Can you sleep at night? Do you have peace with where you are heading?

Sometimes you may need to change the route to navigate new circumstances, like we did when travelling through Africa, if we heard on the radio that there was trouble in an area. Likewise, we also changed from going north to south to south to north as the company we worked for wanted us to work in South Africa first.

1. Are you still on the correct path to achieve your goal?

2. If not, do you want to change your direction to meet the original goal or change your goal to meet the direction?

"Weeping may last for the night – but a shout of joy comes in the morning,"
Psalms 30:5.

"But David encouraged himself in the Lord his God,"
1 Samuel 30:6.

"Keep going, because you did not come this far just to come this far."
unknown

"Develop success from failures. Discouragement and failure are two of the surest stepping stones to success."
-Dale Carnegie

28

Dealing with discouragement

"Don't it make my brown eyes blue,"
Crystal Gayle

Recently I joined an on-line course to learn how to do presentations. We were taught how to do a story braid and the essential elements it had to have to be captivating. The initial five minutes though had to have emotional impact. I chose an incident that had emotionally devastated me and even though it was eight years ago, I still found it hard to write about. I submitted it to my peers and the teachers on the Facebook page and I had some lovely responses to the passion, etc. But I decided that it was too depressing, so I wrote another one. This time, I didn't get any comments which I was a bit disgruntled at as I had spent a lot of time commenting on everyone else's. I decided to write a third one with a completely different story line and this time I tagged a lot of the people whose work I had reviewed. Well, there is definitely truth in that adage, "Be careful what you ask for!" This time, I received an amazing number of comments back but unfortunately, most people didn't like it, and gave me a lot of constructive criticism. As I read each one of the comments, I felt my spirits going lower and lower. By the time I got to the end of them, I was very discouraged; I had thought it quite good, but obviously I was virtually alone in this. I went to bed that night wondering what I was going to do, I felt so discouraged. The next day, I didn't want to go anywhere near it, and so ignored it until the evening, when I decided to look at it again. This time, I decided to change my attitude and to look at it as a learning exercise, after all, the reason for doing the course was to learn. This time, it was a completely different experience. None of the comments had been spiteful or nasty, they had all been constructive (even if I didn't like the criticism) and when I looked at them in humility (rather than the prideful eyes of "I must be right, what's wrong with them"), I saw that the vast majority of comments were valid (oops) and in fact I was very impressed at the time and effort that some people had taken to comment on my work. I decided to swallow my pride and do a fourth version, including everyone's comments. When I posted version four, the results couldn't have been more different. I felt so much happier with it, and everyone was impressed that I'd taken notice of what they had suggested.

Whilst this could seem only a minor discourage-ment to what you are going through, the lessons learnt may help you. These were:

1. It's important to acknowledge that you are discouraged because things didn't go the way that you wanted (that's fine).

2. Get some sleep. If you are tired, everything always seems worse, and fatigue can often be a cause of discouragement in itself.

3. Watch your thoughts, it's okay to be down occasionally, but don't go for an extended "pity party" with a "poor me" attitude, as it can lead to depression.

4. If it's criticism that has upset you, then stand back and try to look at it objectively. Firstly, if it is criticism about your work, then try and divorce that from yourself. It is not you that they are criticizing, just what you did, i.e. just because you may have failed at doing something, does not make you a failure. Also try to look at it objectively and see if their criticism was valid; can you learn anything from their comments that would make you better at your job, or better as a person? Check that it's not just your pride/ ego that has been hurt.

Here are some other tips:

5. Go for a brisk walk, or other aerobic exercise. This will reduce your stress levels and release some endorphins to make you feel better.

6. Ask yourself, "Can I grow from this experience?"

7. Go and watch your favorite comedy movie/series to cheer yourself up ("A merry heart doeth good like a medicine," Proverbs 17:22).

8. Talk about it with a good friend (A problem shared is a problem halved).

9. Speak affirming words/scriptures over and to yourself in the mirror. (See Appendix 3)

10. Ask yourself how your 'hero/heroine in your field' would see this. If you are a Christian, then ask God to show you His view of it.

11. If it is something other than criticism, e.g. a business deal fell through, then ask yourself what practical steps you can do to:

    a. Retrieve the situation or

    b. How to do it differently next time, learn from it.

12. Another cause of discouragement is feeling overwhelmed, maybe a few things have hit you all at the same time. Do something that will give you a quick win, tidy your desk or do the filing.

1. Try and stand back from the discouragement and analyze why you are discouraged (or ask an honest friend to help you analyze it).

2. Ask yourself what can you learn from the situation, how can you improve it?

3. Make a list of everything that you are grateful for (I have included my list in Appendix 6).

Epilogue

T hank you for taking this journey with me through various emotions and lessons that I've learned as I have undertaken my dreams. Whilst I wrote *Passionate Pursuit*, I seemed to go through each of the stages all over again, but now I can say as the book goes out to be published, that it was worth it. I hope that you have enjoyed the book, but more than that, I hope that it has inspired you to take the steps to start out on your own dream/goal.

If it has, I would love to hear about your dream journey and how *Passionate Pursuit* helped.

Or if you think that there should have been other areas/topics that you would have liked to have seen in *Passionate Pursuit*, again, let me know. You can leave your comments at: www.mjspanswick.com.

Also, at the website you can find editable dream questionnaire forms and road maps as well as a larger list of emotions. You will also see photos from our various dreams, including some of the chateau renovation, and details of how to rent the six-bedroom tower (sleeps twelve, self-catering accommodation).

If you think you need a little more help with your dream, I will also be starting a seven-week video course where I go a little deeper into topics and it also includes weekly coaching sessions. Again, details of availability can be found at: www.mjspanswick.com.

By following my dreams and my career, the paths have now converged into the path of my destiny as I start a new life helping others to start and complete their life's dreams and missions. I didn't realize this when I set out to accomplish my dreams, I did them because I thought they would be fun, or a challenge or to help others, but now looking back, I see a divine purpose in it all. So, if you have a dream, then go for it, as it may just be the first stepping stone to your calling and destiny.

Good Luck and God Bless,
Mary-Jo
x

Appendices

Appendix 1

Dream Goal Questionnaire

1. Write out as fully as you can, what your dream is.

2. How long have you had your dream?

3. Why is that your dream?

4. How badly do you want this dream to succeed?

5. What is the purpose of your dream? (i.e. enjoyment/help others/new lifestyle)

6. What do you think you will enjoy most about your dream?

7. What will be the measure of success of your dream? (How will you know you have achieved it?)

8. Will you be doing this dream on your own or with others?

9. If with others:

    a. Are they family/ friends or a business partner?

b. If not family, how long have you known them?

c. Do you have the same goal as one another?

d. Do you have the same life values as one another?

e. Have you ever had to resolve a conflict between you? How did that go?

10. Is your dream a short term/one off event, e.g. driving through Africa, or is it a long term/life-changing dream (starting a business)?

11. How long will your dream take to implement?

a. 3-6 months

b. 6-12 months

c. 1-5 years

d. 5 years +

12. Do you have a fixed start or end date for your dream? If so, what is it?

13. Is your dream just for pleasure or do you intend to make a living out of it?

14. Will you be giving up paid employment to implement your dream?

15. Have you assessed the financial impact of your dream?

16. To implement your dream, will you have to spend time away from your family?

17. Have you assessed any emotional impact of your dream?

18. What do you think is your main stumbling block to starting?

    a. Fear?

    b. Don't know where to start?

    c. Lack of time?

    d. Lack of funds?

19. What is your biggest fear when it comes to your dream?

20. Now that you have answered all of the above questions, look at your answers and turn your dream into a goal by using the following format (I will use our drive though Africa as an example).

My dream is to (*drive all the way from Cape Agulas, South Africa, back to the UK, stopping and visiting countries on the way*), **I will do this with** (*my husband*). **The dream will start** (*once we finish our work assignment in South Africa*) **and will take** (*approximately one year*) **to achieve. I want to do this dream because** (*I think it will be really enjoyable to travel and experience different cultures*). **This dream will be considered a success if** (*we arrive home safely together having driven all the way*).

Appendix 2
Dream Mind Map

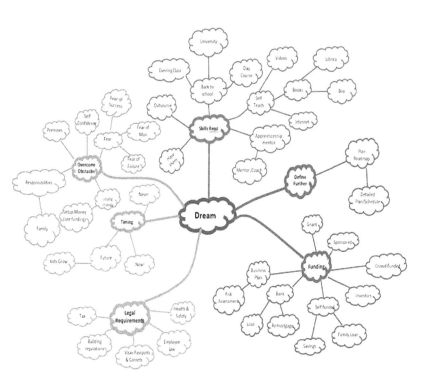

Appendix 3a
Positive Affirmations

Choose your favourites and speak them out loud over yourself until you believe them and they become natural to you.

1. I can do this.

2. I am courageous.

3. I am capable and worthy of success.

4. I will get to where I want to be.

5. I will enjoy the journey of getting to my goal.

6. Today is blessed and fruitful.

7. I am productive.

8. I am intelligent.

9. I am bigger than this problem.

10. I am excited about what today will bring.

11. I am loved.

12. I accept myself physically.

13. My happiness is my choice, and I choose to be happy.

14. I believe in myself.

15. I am creating new adventures and new opportunities.

16. Every day brings me closer to my goals.

17. I am open to new adventures.

18. I have confidence in my skills and abilities.

19. I am strong, physically, mentally and emotionally.

20. I am smart and confident.

21. I am brave and fearless.

22. Nothing is going to stop me from achieving my goal.

23. Today I will learn something new.

24. I will be true to myself.

25. I am grateful for all that I have.

26. I believe that things will work out for the best.

27. I am looking forward to this day.

28. Good things are going to come.

29. I take responsibility for my thoughts.

30. Opportunities are everywhere for me.

Appendix 3b
Affirming Scriptures

1. And we know that God causes all things to work together for good to those who love God, to those who are called according to His purpose. Romans 8:28

2. Therefore, there is now no condemnation for those who are in Christ Jesus. Romans 8:1

3. For you have not received a spirit of slavery leading to fear again, but you have received a spirit of adoption as sons by which we cry out, "Abba! Father!" The Spirit Himself testifies with our spirit that we are children of God. Romans 8:15-16

4. And these whom He predestined, He also called; and these whom He called, He also justified; and these whom He justified, He also glorified. Romans 8:30

5. What then shall we say to these things? If God is for us, who *is* against us? Romans 8:31

6. But in all these things we overwhelm-ingly conquer through Him who loved us. Romans 8:37

7. For I am convinced that neither death, nor life, nor angels, nor principalities, nor things present, nor things to come, nor powers, nor height, nor depth, nor any other cre-ated thing, will be able to separate us from the love of God, which is in Christ Jesus our Lord. Romans 8:38-39

8. "For I know the plans that I have for you," declares the Lord, "plans for welfare and not for calamity to give you a future and a hope." Jeremiah 29:11

9. Then my enemies will turn back in the day when I call; This I know, that God is for me. Psalms 56:9

10. I can do all things through Him who strengthens me. Philippians 4:13

11. But as many as received Him, to them He gave the right to become children of God, even to those who believe in His name. John 1:12

12. But I have called you friends, for all things that I have heard from My Father I have made known to you. John 15:15

13. No man will be able to stand before you all the days of your life. Just as I have been with Moses, I will be with you; I will not fail you or forsake you. Joshua 1:5

14. Be strong and courageous, for you shall give this people possession of the land which I swore to their fathers to give them. Joshua 1:6

15. Only be strong and very courageous; be careful to do according to all the law which Moses My servant commanded you; do not turn from it to the right or to the left, so that you may have success wherever you go. Joshua 1:7

16. And in Him you have been made complete. Colossians 2:10

17. For I am confident of this very thing, that He who began a good work in you will perfect it until the day of Christ Jesus. Philippians 1:6

18. You did not choose Me but I chose you, and appointed you that you would go and bear fruit, and that your fruit would remain, so that whatever you ask of the Father in My name He may give to you. John 15:16

19. Yet those who wait for the Lord will gain new strength; They will mount up *with* wings like eagles, they will run and not get tired, They will walk and not become weary. Isaiah 40:31

20. When you pass through the waters, I will be with you; And through the rivers, they will not overflow you. When you walk through the fire, you will not be scorched, nor will the flame burn you. Isaiah 43:2

21. Have I not commanded you? Be strong and courageous! Do not tremble or be dismayed, for the Lord your God is with you wherever you go. Joshua 1:9

22. The Lord is the one who goes ahead of you; He will be with you. He will not fail you or forsake you. Do not fear or be dismayed. Deuteronomy 31:8

23. Come to Me, all who are weary and heavy-laden, and I will give you rest. Matthew 11:28

24. Look at the birds of the air, that they do not sow, nor reap nor gather into barns, and *yet* your heavenly Father feeds them. Are you not worth much more than they? Matthew 6:26

25. Therefore, my beloved brethren, be steadfast, immovable, always abounding in the work of the Lord, knowing that your toil is not in vain in the Lord. 1 Corinthians 15:58

26. I will lift up my eyes to the mountains; From where shall my help come? My help comes from the Lord, who made heaven and earth.

27. The name of the Lord is a strong tower; The righteous runs into it and is safe. Proverbs 18:10

28. God is our refuge and strength, a very present help in trouble. Psalms 46:1

29. For You formed my inward parts; You wove me in my mother's womb. I will give thanks to You, for I am fearfully and wonderfully

made; Wonderful are Your works, and my soul knows it very well. Psalms 139:12-14

30. Strength and dignity are her clothing, and she smiles at the future. Proverbs 31:25.

Appendix 4
Road Map

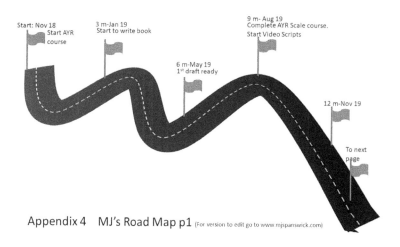

Start: Nov 18
Start AYR course

3 m-Jan 19
Start to write book

9 m- Aug 19
Complete AYR Scale course.
Start Video Scripts

6 m-May 19
1st draft ready

12 m-Nov 19

To next page

Appendix 4   MJ's Road Map p1 (For version to edit go to www.mjspanswick.com)

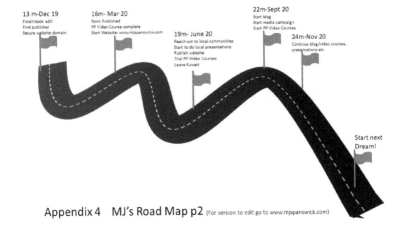

13 m-Dec 19
Finish book edit
Find publisher
Secure website domain

16m- Mar 20
Book Published
PP Video Course complete
Start Website: www.mjspanswick.com

19m- June 20
Reach out to local communities
Start to do local presentations
Publish website
Trial PP Video Courses
Leave Kuwait

22m-Sept 20
Start blog
Start media campaign
Start PP Video Courses

24m-Nov 20
Continue blog/video courses,
presentations etc.

Start next
Dream!

Appendix 4   MJ's Road Map p2 (For version to edit go to www.mjspanswick.com)

Appendix 5
David and Goliath

1 Samuel 17 New American Standard Bible (NASB)

Now the Philistines gathered their armies for battle; and they were gathered at Socoh which belongs to Judah, and they camped between Socoh and Azekah, in Ephes-dammim. Saul and the men of Israel were gathered and camped in the valley of Elah, and drew up in battle array to encounter the Philistines. The Philistines stood on the mountain on one side while Israel stood on the mountain on the other side, with the valley between them. Then a champion came out from the armies of the Philistines named Goliath, from Gath, whose height was six cubits and a span. He had a bronze helmet on his head, and he was clothed with scale-armor which weighed five thousand shekels of bronze. He also had bronze greaves on his legs and a bronze javelin slung between his shoulders. The shaft of his spear was like a weaver's beam, and the head of his spear weighed six hundred shekels of iron; his shield-carrier also walked before him. He stood and shouted to the ranks of Israel and said to them, "Why do you come out to draw up in battle array? Am I not the Philistine and you servants of Saul? Choose a man for yourselves and let him come down to me. If he is able to fight with me and kill me, then we will become your servants; but if I prevail against him and kill him, then you shall become our servants and serve us." Again the Philistine said, "I defy the ranks of Israel this day; give me a man that we may fight together." When Saul and all Israel heard these words of the Philistine, they were dismayed and greatly afraid.

Now David was the son of the Ephrathite of Bethlehem in Judah, whose name was Jesse, and he had eight sons. And Jesse was old in the days of Saul, advanced in years among men. The three older sons of Jesse had gone after Saul to the battle. And the names of his three sons who went to the battle were Eliab the firstborn, and the second to him Abinadab, and the third Shammah. David was the youngest. Now the three oldest followed Saul, but David went back and forth from Saul to tend his father's flock at Bethlehem. The Philistine came forward morning and evening for forty days and took his stand.

Then Jesse said to David his son, "Take now for your brothers an ephah of this roasted grain and these ten loaves and run to the camp to your brothers. Bring also these ten cuts of cheese to the commander of their thousand, and look into the welfare of your brothers, and bring back news of them. For Saul and they and all the men of Israel are in the valley of Elah, fighting with the Philistines." So David arose early in the morning and left the flock with a keeper and took the supplies and went as Jesse had commanded him. And he came to the circle of the camp while the army was going out in battle array shouting the war cry. Israel and the Philistines drew up in battle array, army against army. Then David left his baggage in the care of the baggage keeper, and ran to the battle line and entered in order to greet his brothers. As he was talking with them, behold, the champion, the Philistine from Gath named Goliath, was coming up from the army of the Philistines, and he spoke these same words; and David heard them.

When all the men of Israel saw the man, they fled from him and were greatly afraid. The men of Israel said, "Have you seen this man who is coming up? Surely he is coming up to defy Israel. And it will be that the king will enrich the man who kills him with great riches and will give him his daughter and make his father's house free in Israel."

Then David spoke to the men who were standing by him, saying, "What will be done for the man who kills this Philistine and takes away the reproach from Israel? For who is this uncircumcised Philistine, that he should taunt the armies of the living God?" The people answered him in accord with this word, saying, "Thus it will be done for the man who kills him."

Now Eliab his oldest brother heard when he spoke to the men; and Eliab's anger burned against David and he said, "Why have you come down? And with whom have you left those few sheep in the wilderness? I know your insolence and the wickedness of your heart; for you have come down in order to see the battle." But David said, "What have I done now? Was it not just a question?" Then he turned away from him to another and said the same thing; and the people answered the same thing as before. When the words which David spoke were heard, they told them to Saul, and he sent for him. David said to Saul, "Let no man's heart fail on account of him; your servant will go and fight with this Philistine." Then Saul said to David, "You are not able to go against this Philistine to fight with him; for you are but a youth while he has been a warrior from his youth." But David said to Saul, "Your servant was tending his father's sheep. When a lion or a bear came and took a lamb from the flock, I went out after him and attacked him, and rescued it from his mouth; and when he rose up against me, I seized him by his beard and struck him and killed him. Your servant has killed both the lion and the bear; and this uncircumcised Philistine will be like one of them, since he has taunted the armies of the living God." And David said, "The Lord who delivered me from the paw of the lion and from the paw of the bear, He will deliver me from the hand of this Philistine." And Saul said to David, "Go, and may the Lord be with you." Then Saul clothed David with his garments and put a bronze helmet on his head, and he clothed him with armor. David girded his sword over his armor and tried to walk, for he had not tested them. So David said to Saul, "I cannot go with these, for I have not tested them." And David took them off. He took his stick in his hand and chose for himself five smooth stones from the brook, and put them in the shepherd's bag which he had, even in his pouch, and his sling was in his hand; and he approached the Philistine. Then the Philistine came on and approached David, with the shield-bearer in front of him. When the Philistine looked and saw David, he disdained him; for he was but a youth, and ruddy, with a handsome appearance. The Philistine said to David, "Am I a dog, that you come to me with sticks?" And the Philistine cursed David by his gods. The Philistine also said to David, "Come to me, and I will give your flesh to the birds of the sky and the beasts of the field." Then David said to the Philistine, "You come to me with a sword, a spear and a javelin, but I come to you in the name of the Lord of hosts, the God of the armies of Israel, whom you have taunted. This day the Lord will deliver you up into my hands, and I will strike you down and remove your head from you. And I will give the dead bodies of the army of the Philistines this day to the birds of the sky and the wild beasts of the earth, that all the earth may know that there is a God in Israel, and that all this assembly may know that the Lord does not deliver by sword or by spear; for the battle is the Lord's and He will give you into our hands."

Then it happened when the Philistine rose and came and drew near to meet David, that David ran quickly toward the battle line to meet the Philistine. And David put his hand into his bag and took from it a stone and slung it, and struck the Philistine on his forehead. And the stone sank into his forehead, so that he fell on his face to the ground.

Thus David prevailed over the Philistine with a sling and a stone, and he struck the Philistine and killed him; but there was no sword in David's hand. Then David ran and stood over the Philistine and took his sword and drew it out of its sheath and killed him, and cut off his head with it. When the Philistines saw that their champion was dead, they fled. The men of Israel and Judah arose and shouted and pursued the Philistines as far as the valley, and to the gates of Ekron. And the slain Philistines lay along the way to Shaaraim, even to Gath and Ekron. The sons of Israel returned from chasing the Philistines and plundered their camps. Then David took the Philistine's head and brought it to Jerusalem, but he put his weapons in his tent.

Appendix 6
Thirty Things I Am Grateful For

(In no particular order)

- Life – Being alive!
- My health – Functioning body parts
- Having a roof over my head
- Having enough food to eat
- Sunshine
- Snow falling and fresh on the ground
- My family
- My friends
- Education
- The internet & technology in general
- Jesus/Holy Spirit/Father God
- Lemon cake
- Security – Having a door I can lock
- Beauty in nature

- Colour (so glad we do not live in a mono-chrome world!)
- Clean running water & indoor sanitation
- Glass of wine/Gin & tonic
- Stars in the night sky
- Sleeping on fresh bed sheets
- The affection of pets
- Beautiful architecture
- Cuddles with your partner
- Laughing so much you can't breathe
- Dinner with friends
- An open fire
- Swinging on a swing
- Rainbows
- Religious freedom
- The beauty of sunrises & sunsets
- Clean air to breathe

Appendix 7
List of Forty Emotions

Anger	Hopeful
Anxious	Hurt
Bitter	Inadequate
Bold	Indifferent
Bored	Inferior
Confident	Insecure
Confused	Insignificant
Depressed	Joyful
Determined	Jealous
Disappointed	Lonely
Discouraged	Loved
Disillusioned	Motivated
Exasperated	Overwhelmed
Exhausted	Passionate
Fearful	Regretful
Frightened	Sad
Frustrated	Shameful
Furious	Thankful
Guilty	Undervalued
Happy	Worried

Appendix 8

Schedule/Simple Gantt Chart

For editable version go to www.mjspanswick.com

Appendix 8 - Simple Gantt Chart using Excel (Go to www.mjspanswick.com for native file)

ACTIVITIES	Nov 18	Dec 18	Jan 19	Feb 19	Mar 19	Apr 19	May 19	Jun 19	Jul 19	Aug 19	Sep 19	Oct 19	Nov 19	Dec 19	Jan 20	Feb 20	Mar 20	Apr 20	May 20	Jun 20	Jul 20	Aug 20	Sep 20	Oct 20	Nov 20	Dec 20
Undertake AYR Course																										
Start to write PP book																										
First draft of book complete						☆																				
Edit & Complete book																										
Publish book (others)																										
Undertake Scale Workshop																										
Write PP Video Course																										
Record PP Video Course																										
Purchase website domain										☆																
Create website																										
Sort out software for Video Course																										
Write 45 min Presentation																										
Start blog																										
Social media campaign																										
Reach out to local comunities																										
Start to do local presentations																										
Leave Kuwait																				☆						
Start 1st PP Video Course & Coaching																							☆			
Reach out to presentation organisers																										
Presentations UK/USA/elsewhere																										

	Nov 18	Dec 18	Jan 19	Feb 19	Mar 19	Apr 19	May 19	Jun 19	Jul 19	Aug 19	Sep 19	Oct 19	Nov 19	Dec 19	Jan 20	Feb 20	Mar 20	Apr 20	May 20	Jun 20	Jul 20	Aug 20	Sep 20	Oct 20	Nov 20	Dec 20

TIME

Copyright Acknowledgements

Bible verses quoted from the New American Standard Bible version by the Lockman Foundation

Poem excerpt "The Road Not Taken" by Robert Frost

Poem excerpt "Don't Quit" by John Greenleaf Whittier

Picture of "Little girl & star" by Annabel Emery www.halcyondays.com

Lightning Source UK Ltd.
Milton Keynes UK
UKHW020209280420
362405UK00006B/261